BLOOD
KNOT

and

OTHER PLAYS

BOOKS BY ATHOL FUGARD

AVAILABLE FROM TCG

A Lesson From Aloes
My Children! My Africa!
Notebooks: 1960–1977
The Road to Mecca
Statements

BLOOD KNOT

and

OTHER PLAYS

—

ATHOL
FUGARD

THEATRE COMMUNICATIONS GROUP

1991

Blood Knot and Other Plays is published by
Theatre Communications Group, Inc.,
355 Lexington Ave., New York, NY 10017.

TCG gratefully acknowledges public funds from the National Endowment for the
Arts and the New York State Council on the Arts in addition to the generous
support of the following foundations and corporations: Alcoa Foundation; Amer-
itech Foundation; ARCO Foundation; AT&T Foundation; Citibank; Common
Wealth Fund; ConAgra Charitable Foundation; Consolidated Edison Company
of New York; Nathan Cummings Foundation; Eleanor Naylor Dana Charitable
Trust; Dayton Hudson Foundation; Exxon Corporation; Ford Foundation; James
Irvine Foundation; Jerome Foundation; Andrew W. Mellon Foundation; Metro-
politan Life Foundation; National Broadcasting Company; Pew Charitable
Trusts; Philip Morris Companies; Reed Foundation; Scherman Foundation; Shell
Oil Company Foundation; Shubert Foundation.

Photograph of the author by T. Charles Erickson

Fugard, Athol.
Blood knot, and other plays / Athol Fugard.
Contents: Blood knot—Hello and goodbye—Boesman and Lena.
ISBN 1-55936-019-4 (cloth) ISBN 1-55936-020-8 (paper)
I. Title.
PR9369.3.F8A6   1991
822-dc20
90-29029
CIP

Cover design by The Sarabande Press

First Edition, May 1991

CONTENTS

BLOOD KNOT

The Blood Knot (original title) was first presented in the United
States by Sidney Bernstein and Lucille Lortel at the Cricket
Theatre on March 2, 1964, under the direction of John Berry. Set
design was by John Bury, costume design by Martha Gould and
lighting design by Harold Baldridge. The cast was as follows:

MORRIS .... *J.D. Cannon*
ZACHARIAH .... *James Earl Jones*

The play's world premiere took place at the Rehearsal Room of the
African Music and Drama Association, Johannesburg, South Africa, September 3, 1961, under the author's direction and with the
following cast:

MORRIS .... *Athol Fugard*
ZACHARIAH .... *Zakes Mokae*

The 25th Anniversary Production of the revised *Blood Knot* was
produced by the Yale Repertory Theatre, New Haven, Connecti-
cut, September 17, 1988, also under the author's direction. Sets
were designed by Rusty Smith, costumes by Susan Hilferty and
lights by William B. Warfel. Mr. Fugard and Mr. Mokae recreated
their original roles.

CHARACTERS

MORRIS
ZACHARIAH

Zachariah is dark-skinned and Morris is light-skinned.

All the action takes place in a one-room shack in the "non-white
location" of Korsten, Port Elizabeth. The walls are a patchwork
of scraps of corrugated iron, packing-case wood, flattened cardboard boxes, and old hessian bags. One door, one window (no
curtains), two beds, a table and two chairs. Also in evidence is a
cupboard of sorts with an oil-stove, a kettle and a few pots. The
shack is tidy and swept, but this only enhances the poverty of its
furnishings. Over one of the beds is a shelf on which are a few
books (including a Bible) and an alarm-clock.

SCENE ONE

Late afternoon.

Lying on his bed, the one with the shelf, and staring up at the ceiling, is Morris. *After a few seconds he stands up on the bed, looks at the alarm clock, and then lies down again in the same position. Time passes. The alarm rings and Morris jumps purposefully to his feet. He knows exactly what he is going to do. First, he winds and resets the clock, then lights the oil stove and puts on a kettle of water. Next, he places an enamel washbasin on the floor in front of the other bed and lays out a towel. He feels the kettle on the stove and then goes to the door and looks out. Nothing. He wanders aimlessly around the room for a few more seconds, pausing at the window for a long look at whatever lies beyond. Eventually he is back at the door again and, after a short wait, he sees someone coming. A second burst of activity. He places a packet of footsalts beside the basin and finally replaces the kettle.*

Zachariah comes in through the door. Their meeting is without words. Morris nods and Zachariah grunts on his way to the bed, where he sits down, drags off his shoes, and rolls up his trousers. While he does this, Morris sprinkles footsalts into the basin and then sits back on his haunches and waits. Zachariah dips his feet into the basin, sighs with satisfaction, but stops abruptly when he sees Morris smile. He frowns, pretends to think, and makes a great business of testing the water with his foot.

ZACHARIAH. Not as hot as last night, hey?

MORRIS. Last night you said it was too hot.

ZACHARIAH [*thinks about this*]. That's what I mean.

MORRIS. So what is it? Too hot or too cold?

ZACHARIAH. When?

MORRIS. Now.

ZACHARIAH. Luke-ish. [*Bends forward and smells.*] New stuff?

MORRIS. Yes.

ZACHARIAH. Let's see.

[*Morris hands him the packet. Zachariah first smells it, then takes out a pinch between thumb and forefinger.*]

It's also white.

MORRIS. Yes, but it is different stuff.

3

ZACHARIAH. The other lot was also white, but it didn't help, hey?

MORRIS. This is definitely different stuff, Zach. [*Pointing.*] See. There's the name. Radium Salts.

[*Zachariah is not convinced. Morris fetches a second packet.*]

Here's the other. Schultz's Foot Salts.

ZACHARIAH [*taking the second packet and looking inside*]. They look the same, don't they? [*Smells.*] But they smell different. You know something? I think the old lot smells nicest. What do you say we go back to the old lot?

MORRIS. But you just said it didn't help!

ZACHARIAH. But it smells better, man.

MORRIS. It's not the smell, Zach. You don't go by the smell, man.

ZACHARIAH. No?

MORRIS. No. It's the healing properties.

ZACHARIAH. Oh, maybe.

MORRIS [*taking back the new packet*]. Zach, listen to this . . . [*Reads.*] 'For all agonies of the joints: lumbago, rheumatism, tennis elbows, housemaid's knees; also ideal for bunions, corns, callouses'—that's what you got . . . 'and for soothing irritated skins.'

[*Zachariah lets him finish, examining the old packet while Morris reads.*]

ZACHARIAH. How much that new stuff cost?

MORRIS. Why?

ZACHARIAH. Tell me, man.

MORRIS [*aware of what is coming*]. Listen, Zach. It's the healing properties. Price has nothing . . .

ZACHARIAH [*insistent*]. How—much—does—that—cost?

MORRIS. Twenty-five cents.

ZACHARIAH [*with a small laugh*]. You know something?

MORRIS. Yes, yes, I know what you're going to say.

ZACHARIAH. This old stuff, which isn't so good, is thirty cents. Five cents more! [*He starts to laugh.*]

4

MORRIS So? Listen, Zach. Price . . . ZACH! Do you want to listen or don't you?

[*Zachariah is laughing loud in triumph.*]

PRICE HAS GOT NOTHING TO DO WITH IT!

ZACHARIAH. Then why is this more money?

MORRIS. Profit. He's making more profit on the old stuff. Satisfied?

ZACHARIAH. So?

MORRIS. So.

ZACHARIAH. Oh. [*Slowly.*] So he's making more profit on the old stuff. [*The thought comes.*] But that's what you been buying, man! *Ja*—and with my money, remember! So it happens to be my profit he's making. Isn't that so?

[*He is getting excited and now stands in the basin of water.*]

Hey. I see it now. I do the bloody work—all day long—in the sun. Not him. It's my stinking feet that got the hardnesses. But he goes and makes my profit.

[*Steps out of the basin.*]

I want to work this out, man. How long you been buying that old stuff?

MORRIS. Only four weeks.

ZACHARIAH. Four weeks?

MORRIS. Yes.

ZACHARIAH. That makes four packets, hey? So you say five cents profit . . . which comes to . . . twenty cents . . . isn't that so? Whose? Mine. Who's got it? Him . . . him . . . some dirty, rotting, stinking, creeping, little . . .

MORRIS. But we are buying the cheap salts now, Zach! [*Pause.*] He's not going to get the profits anymore. And what is more still, the new salts is better.

[*The thread of Zachariah's reasoning has been broken. He stares blankly at Morris.*]

ZACHARIAH. I still say the old smells sweeter.

MORRIS. Okay, okay, listen. I tell you what. I'll give you a double dose. One of the old and one of the new . . . together! That way you get the healing properties *and* the smell. Satisfied?

ZACHARIAH. Okay.

[*He goes to the bed, sits down and once again soaks his feet.*]

Hey! You got any more warm, Morrie?

[*Morris pours the last of the hot water into the basin. Zachariah now settles down to enjoy the luxury of his footbath. Morris helps him off with his tie, and afterwards puts away his shoes.*]

MORRIS. How did it go today?

ZACHARIAH. He's got me standing again.

MORRIS. At the gate?

ZACHARIAH. *Ja.*

MORRIS. But didn't you tell him, Zach? I told you to tell him that your feet are calloused and that you wanted to go back to pots.

ZACHARIAH. I did.

MORRIS. And then?

ZACHARIAH. He said: 'Go to the gate or go to hell.'

MORRIS. That's an insult.

ZACHARIAH. What's the other one?

MORRIS. Injury!

ZACHARIAH No, no. The long one.

MORRIS. Inhumanity!

ZACHARIAH. That's it. That's what I think it is. My inhumanity from him. 'Go to the gate or go to hell.' What do they think I am?

MORRIS. What about me?

ZACHARIAH. [*Anger*]. What do *you* think I am?

MORRIS. No, Zach! Good heavens! You got it all wrong. What do *they* think I am, when they think what you are.

ZACHARIAH. Oh.

MORRIS. Yes. I'm on your side, they're on theirs. I mean, I couldn't be living here with you and not be on yours, could I, Zach?

[*Morris is helping Zachariah off with his coat. When Zachariah is not looking, he smells it.*]

Zach, I think we must borrow Minnie's bath again.

ZACHARIAH. Okay, Morrie.

MORRIS. What about me? Do I smell?

ZACHARIAH. No. [*Pause.*] Hey! Have I started again?

[*Morris doesn't answer. Zachariah laughs.*]

Hey! What's that thing you say, Morrie? The one about smelling?

MORRIS [*quoting*]. 'The rude odours of manhood.'

ZACHARIAH. 'The rude odours of manhood.' What's the other one? The long one?

MORRIS. 'No smell'?

[*Zachariah nods.*]

> 'No smell doth stink as sweet as labour.
> 'Tis joyous times when man and man
> Do work and sweat in common toil,
> When all the world's my neighbour.'

ZACHARIAH. 'When all the world's my neighbour.'

[*Zachariah starts drying his feet with the towel. Morris empties the basin and puts it away.*]

Minnie.

MORRIS. What about Minnie?

ZACHARIAH. Our neighbour. You know, strange thing about Minnie. He doesn't come no more.

MORRIS. I don't miss him.

ZACHARIAH. No, you don't remember, man. I'm talking about before you. He came every night. *Ja!* Me and him used to go out—together, you know—quite a bit. [*Pause.*] Hey! How did I forget a thing like that!

MORRIS. What are you talking about?

ZACHARIAH. Me and Minnie going out! Almost every night . . . and I've forgotten. [*Pause.*] How long you been here, Morrie?

MORRIS. Oh, about a year now, Zach.

ZACHARIAH. Only one miserable year and I have forgotten just like that! Just like it might not have never happened!

MORRIS. Yes, Zach, the year has flown by.

ZACHARIAH. You never want to go out, Morrie.

MORRIS. So I don't want to go out. Ask me why and I'll

tell you. Come on.

ZACHARIAH. Why?

MORRIS. Because we got plans, remember? We're saving for a future, which is something Minnie didn't have.

ZACHARIAH. *Ja.* He doesn't come no more.

MORRIS. You said that already, Zach. I heard you the first time.

ZACHARIAH. I was just thinking. I remembered him today. I was at the gate. It was lunchtime, and I was eating my bread.

MORRIS. Hey—did you like the peanut butter sandwiches I made?

ZACHARIAH. I was eating my bread, and then it comes, the thought: What the hell has happened to old Minnie?

MORRIS. Zach, I was asking you—

ZACHARIAH. Wait, man! I'm remembering it now. He used to come, I thought to myself, with his guitar to this room, to me, to his friend, old Zachariah, waiting for him here. Friday nights it was, when an *ou*'s got pay in his pocket and there's no work tomorrow and Minnie's coming. Now there was a friend for a man! He could laugh, could Minnie, and drink! He knew the spots, I'm telling you . . . the places to be, the good times . . . and—*Ja!* [*Reverently.*] Minnie had music. Listen, he could do a *vastrap*, that man, non-stop, on all strings at once. He knew the lot. Polka, tickey-*draai, opskud en uitkap, ek sê* . . . Now that was jollification for you, with Minnie coming around. So, when I'm waiting in here, and I hear that guitar in the street, at my door, I'm happy! 'It's you!' I shout. He stops. 'I know it's you,' I say. He pretends he isn't there, you see. 'Minnie,' I call. 'Minnie!' So what does he do? He gives me a quick *chick-a-doem* in G. He knows I like G. 'It's Friday night, Minnie.' '*Chick-a-doem-doem, doem, doem,*' he says. And then I'm laughing. 'You bugger! You motherless bastard!' So I open the door. What do I see? Minnie! And what's he got in his hand? Golden Moments at fifty cents a bottle. Out there, Morrie, standing just right on that spot in the street with his bottle and his music and laughing with me. 'Zach,' he says, '*Ou pellie*, tonight is the night—' [*The alarm goes off.*] . . . is the night . . . is the night . . . is the night . . .

[*Zachariah loses the thread of his story. By the time the alarm stops, he has forgotten what he was saying. The moment the alarm goes off, Morris springs to his feet and busies himself at the table with their supper. Zachariah eventually goes back to the bed.*]

MORRIS [*watching Zachariah surreptitiously from the table*]. I been thinking, Zach. It's time we started making some definite plans. I mean . . . we've agreed on the main idea. The thing now is to find the right place. [*Pause.*] Zach? [*Pause.*] We have agreed, haven't we?

ZACHARIAH. About what?

MORRIS. Hell, man. The future. Is it going to be a small two-man farm, just big enough for me and you; or what is it going to be?

ZACHARIAH. *Ja.*

MORRIS. Right. We agree. Now, I'm saying we got to find the right place. [*Pause.*] Zach! What's the matter with you tonight?

ZACHARIAH. I was trying to remember what I was saying about Minnie. There was something else.

MORRIS. Now listen, Zach! You said yourself he doesn't come no more. So what are you doing thinking about him? Here am I putting our future to you and you don't even listen. The farm, Zach! Remember, man? The things we're going to do. Picture it! Picking our own fruit. Chasing those damned baboons helter-skelter in the *koppies*. Chopping the firewood trees . . . and a cow . . . and a horse . . . and little chickens. Isn't that exciting? Well, I haven't been sitting still.

[*Morris fetches an old map from the shelf over his bed.*]

Here, I want to show you something. You want to know what it is? A map . . . of Africa. Now, this is the point, Zach. Look—there . . . and there . . . and down here . . . Do you see it? Blank. Large, blank spaces. Not a town, not a road, not even those thin little red lines. And, notice, they're green. That means grass. I reckon we should be able to get a few acres in one of these blank spaces for next to nothing.

[*Zachariah, bored, goes to the window and looks out.*]

You listening, Zach?

ZACHARIAH. *Ja.*

MORRIS. This is not just talk, you know. It's serious. One fine day, you wait and see. We'll pack our things in something and get the hell and gone out of here. You say I don't want to get out? My reply is that I do, but I want to get right out. You think I like it here more than you? You should have been here this afternoon, Zach. The wind was blowing again. Coming this way it was, right across the lake. You should have smelt it, man. I'm telling you that water has gone bad. Really rotten! And what about the factories there on the other side? Hey? Lavatories all around us? They've left no room for a man to breathe in this world. But when we go, Zach, together, and we got a place to go, our farm in the future . . . that will be different.

[*Zachariah has been at the window all the time, staring out. He now sees something which makes him laugh. Just a chuckle to begin with, but with a suggestion of lechery.*]

What's so funny?

ZACHARIAH. Come here.

MORRIS. What's there?

ZACHARIAH. Two donkeys, man. You know.

[*Morris makes no move to the window. Zachariah stays there, laughing from time to time.*]

MORRIS. Yes. It's not just talk. When you bring your pay home tomorrow and we put away the usual, guess what we will have, Zach? Go on, guess. Forty-five rands. If it wasn't for me you wouldn't have nothing. Ever think about that? You talk about going out, but forty-five rands—

ZACHARIAH [*breaking off in the middle of a laugh*]. Hey! I remember now! By hell! About Minnie. [*His voice expresses vast disbelief.*] How did I forget a thing like that? It was . . . ja . . . ja . . . It was a woman! That's what we had when we went out at night. Woman!

[*Morris doesn't move. He stares at Zachariah blankly. When the latter pauses for a second, Morris speaks again in an almost normal voice.*]

MORRIS. Supper's ready.

[*Zachariah loses the train of his thought, as with the alarm clock, earlier. Morris sits down.*]

So . . . where were we? Yes. Our plans. When, Zach? That's the next thing we got to think about. Should we take our

chance with a hundred rands, one hundred and fifty? I mean
. . . we could even wait till there is three hundred, isn't that so?

[*Morris has already started on his supper. As if hypnotized by the
sound of the other man's voice Zachariah fetches a chair and sits.*]

So what are we going to do, you ask? This. Find out what the
deposit, cash, on a small two-man farm, in one of those blank
spaces, is. Take some bread, man. [*Offering a slice.*]

ZACHARIAH. No! [*Hurls his slice of bread into a corner of the shack.*]

MORRIS. What's this?

[*Zachariah sweeps away the plate of food in front of him.*]
Zach!

ZACHARIAH. You're not going to make me forget. I won't. I'm
not going to. We had woman I tell you. [*Pounding the table with
his fists.*] Woman! Woman! Woman!

MORRIS. Do you still want the farm?

ZACHARIAH. Shut up! I won't listen.

[*Jumps up and rushes across to the other side of the room where his
jacket is hanging, and begins to put it on.*]

What do you think I am, hey? Two legs and trousers. I'm a
man. And in this world there is also woman, and the one has
got to get the other. Even donkeys know that. What I want to
know now, right this very now, is why me, Zach, a man, for a
whole miserable year has had none. I was doing all right
before that, wasn't I? Minnie used to come. He had a bottle, or
I had a bottle, but we both had a good time, for a long time.
And then you came . . . and then . . . and then . . . [*Pause.*]

MORRIS. Go on . . . say it.

ZACHARIAH. . . . . then you came. That's all.

[*Zachariah's violence is ebbing away. Perplexity takes its place.*]

You knocked on the door. Friday night. I remember, I got a
fright. A knocking on my door on Friday night? On my door?
Who? Not Minnie. Minnie's coming all right, but not like
that. So I had a look, and it was you standing there, and you
said something, hey? What did I say? 'Come in.' Didn't I?
'Come in,' I said. And when we had eaten I said, 'Come out
with me and a friend of mine, called Minnie.' Then you said:
'Zach, let us spend tonight talking.' *Ja*, that's it. That's all. A

whole year of spending tonights talking, talking. I'm sick of talking. I'm sick of this room.

MORRIS. I know, Zach. [*He speaks quietly, soothingly.*] That's why we got plans for the future.

ZACHARIAH. But I was in here ten years without plans and never needed them!

MORRIS. Time, Zach. It passes.

ZACHARIAH. I was in here ten years and didn't worry about my feet, or a future, or having supper on time! But I had fun and Minnie's music!

MORRIS. That's life for you, Zach. The passing of time, and worthless friends.

ZACHARIAH. I want woman.

MORRIS. I see. I see that, Zach. Believe me, I do. But let me think about it. Okay? Now have some supper and I'll think about it.

[*Morris puts his own plate of food in front of Zachariah and then moves around the room picking up the food that Zachariah swept to the floor.*]

You get fed up with talking, I know, Zach. But it helps, man. [*At the window.*] You find the answers to things, like we are going to find the answer to your problem. I mean . . . look what it's done for us already. Our plans! Our future! You should be grateful, man. And remember what I said. You're not the only one who's sick of this room. It also gets me down. [*Turning to Zachariah, leaving the window.*] Have you noticed, Zach, the days are getting shorter, the nights longer? Autumn is in our smelly air. It's the time I came back, hey! About a year ago! We should have remembered what day it was, though. Would have made a good birthday, don't you think? A candle on a cake for the day that Morris came back to Zach.

[*Zachariah leaves the table and goes to his bed.*]

You finished?

ZACHARIAH. *Ja.*

MORRIS. [*Pause. Morris makes the sandwiches.*] Has it helped, Zach?

ZACHARIAH. What?

MORRIS. The talking.

ZACHARIAH. Helped what?

MORRIS. About . . . woman.

ZACHARIAH. It's still there, Morrie. You said you was going to think about it and me.

MORRIS. I'm still busy, Zach. It takes time. Shall I talk some more?

ZACHARIAH. Let me!

[*He speaks eagerly. The first sign of life since the outburst.*]

Let me talk about . . . woman.

MORRIS. You think it wise?

ZACHARIAH. You said it helps. I want to help.

MORRIS. Go on.

ZACHARIAH. You know what I was remembering, Morrie? As I sat there?

MORRIS. No.

ZACHARIAH. Guess.

MORRIS. I can't.

ZACHARIAH. [*Soft, nostalgic smile.*] The first one. My very first one. You was already gone. It was in those years. [*Sigh.*] Her name was Connie.

MORRIS. That's a lovely name, Zach.

ZACHARIAH. Connie Ferreira.

MORRIS. You were happy, hey?

ZACHARIAH. *Ja.*

MORRIS. Don't be shy. Tell me more.

ZACHARIAH. We were young. Her mother did the washing. Connie used to buy blue soap from the Chinaman on the corner.

MORRIS. Your sweetheart, hey!

ZACHARIAH. I waited for her.

MORRIS. Was it true love?

ZACHARIAH. She called me a black *hotnot*, the bitch, so I waited for her. She had tits like fruits and I was waiting in the bushes.

MORRIS [*absolute loss of interest*]. Yes, Zach.

13

ZACHARIAH. She was coming along alone. Hell! Don't I remember Connie now! Coming along alone she was and I was waiting in the bushes. [*Laugh*.] She got a fright, she did. She tried to fight, to bite . . .

MORRIS. All right, Zach!

ZACHARIAH. She might have screamed, but when I had her . . .

MORRIS. All right, Zach! [*Pause*.]

ZACHARIAH. That was Connie. [*He broods*.]

MORRIS. Feeling better?

ZACHARIAH. A little.

MORRIS. Talking helps, doesn't it? I said so. You find the answers to things.

ZACHARIAH. Talking to one would help me even more.

MORRIS. [*Pause*.] You mean to a woman?

ZACHARIAH. I'm telling you, Morrie, I really mean it, man. With all my heart.

MORRIS [*the idea is coming*]. There's a thought there, Zach.

ZACHARIAH. There is?

MORRIS. In fact I think I've got it.

ZACHARIAH. What?

MORRIS. The answer to your problem.

ZACHARIAH. Woman?

MORRIS. That's it! You said talking to one would help you, didn't you? So what about writing? Just as good, isn't it, if she writes back?

ZACHARIAH. Who . . . who you talking about?

MORRIS. A pen-pal. Zach! A corresponding pen-pal of the opposite sex! Don't you know them? [*Zachariah's face is blank*.] It's a woman, you see! [*Looking for newspaper*.] She wants a man friend, but she's in another town, so she writes to him—to you!

ZACHARIAH. No, I don't know her.

MORRIS. You will. You're her pen-pal!

ZACHARIAH. I don't write letters.

MORRIS. I will write them for you.

14

ZACHARIAH. Then it's your pen-pal.

MORRIS. No, Zach. You tell me what to say. You see, she writes to you. She doesn't even know about me. Can't you see it, man? A letter to Mr Zachariah Pietersen—from her.

ZACHARIAH. I don't read letters.

MORRIS. I'll read them to you.

ZACHARIAH. From a woman.

MORRIS. From a woman. You can take your pick.

ZACHARIAH [*now really interested*]. Hey!

MORRIS. There's so many.

ZACHARIAH. Is that so!

MORRIS. Big ones, small ones.

ZACHARIAH. What do you know about that!

MORRIS. Young ones, old ones.

ZACHARIAH. No. Not the old ones, Morrie. [*Excited.*] The young ones, on the small side.

MORRIS. Just take your pick.

ZACHARIAH. Okay. I will.

MORRIS. Now listen, Zach. When you get your pay tomorrow, go to a shop and ask for a newspaper with pen-pals.

ZACHARIAH. With pen-pals.

MORRIS. That's it. We'll study them and you can make your pick.

ZACHARIAH. And I can say what I like? Hey! What do you know! Pen-pals!

[*The alarm-clock rings.*]

Pen-pals!

[*Zachariah flops back on his bed laughing. Morris drifts to the window.*]

MORRIS. Wind's coming up. You sleepy?

ZACHARIAH. It's been a long day.

MORRIS. Okay, I'll cut it short. Your turn to choose the reading tonight, Zach.

[*Morris fetches the Bible from the shelf over his bed. He hands it to Zachariah who, with his eyes tightly closed, opens it and brings his finger down on the page.*]

Four?

[*Zachariah nods. Morris reads.*]

'And if thou bring an oblation of a meat offering baken in the oven, it shall be unleavened cakes of fine flour mingled with oil, or unleavened wafers anointed with oil; and if thy oblation be a meat offering baken in a pan, it shall be of fine flour, unleavened, mingled with oil. Thou shalt part it in pieces and pour oil thereon. It is a meat offering.'

ZACHARIAH. Sounds nice, hey?

MORRIS. You need an oven, Zach. Think of those you love. Ask for what you really want.

ZACHARIAH. Dear God, please bring back Minnie.

MORRIS. Is that all?

ZACHARIAH. Amen.

[*Morris replaces the Bible, finds needle and cotton, and then takes Zachariah's coat to the table.*]

MORRIS. I'm helping you, aren't I, Zach?

ZACHARIAH. *Ja.*

MORRIS. I want to believe that. You see . . . [*Pause.*] There was all those years, when I was away.

ZACHARIAH. Why did you come back?

MORRIS. I was passing this way.

ZACHARIAH. So why did you stay?

MORRIS. We are brothers, remember.

[*A few seconds pass in silence. Morris threads his needle and then starts working on a tear in Zachariah's coat.*]

That's a word, hey! Brothers! There's a broody sound for you if ever there was. I mean . . . take the others. Father. What is there for us in . . . Father? We never knew him. Even Mother. She died and we were young. That's the trouble with 'Mother'. We never said it enough.

[*He tries it.*]

Mother. Mother! Yes. Just a touch of sadness in it, and a grey dress on Sundays, soapsuds on brown hands. That's the lot. Father, Mother, and the sisters we haven't got. But brothers! Try it. Brotherhood. Brother-in-arms, each other's arms.

Brotherly love. That's a big one, hey, Zach? Zach?

[*He looks at Zachariah's bed.*]

Zachie? Zachariah!

[*He is asleep. Morris takes the lamp, goes to the bed, and looks down at the sleeping man. He returns to the table, picks up the Bible and after an inward struggle speaks in a solemn, 'Sunday' voice.*]

'And he said, what hast thou done? The voice of thy brother's blood crieth unto me from the ground. And now art thou cursed from the earth, which hath opened her mouth to receive thy brother's blood from thy hand. When thou tillest the ground it shall not henceforth yield unto thee her strength, a fugitive and a vagabond shalt thou be in the earth.'

[*Pause.*]

Oh Lord, Lord. So I turned around on the road, and came back. About this time, a year ago. It could have been today. I remember turning off the road and heading this way. I thought: it looks the same. It was. Because when I reached the first *pondokkies* and the thin dogs, the wind turned and brought the stink from the lake. No one recognized me after all those years. I could see they weren't sure, and wanting to say 'Sir' when I asked them the way. Six down, they said, pointing to the water's edge. So then there was only time left for a few short thoughts between counting doors. Will he be home? Will I be welcome? Be forgiven? Be brave, Morris! I held my breath . . . knocked . . . and waited . . .

[*Pause.*]

You were wearing this old coat . . .

[*Morris puts on Zachariah's coat. It is several sizes too large.*]

It's been a big help to me, this warm, old coat. You get right inside a man when you can wrap up in the smell of him. It prepared me for your flesh, Zach. Because your flesh, you see, has an effect on me. The sight of it, the feel of it . . . It feels, you see . . . I saw you again after all those years . . . and it hurt, man.

SCENE TWO

The next evening.

Zachariah sits disconsolately on the bed, his feet in the basin. Morris is studying a newspaper.

MORRIS. Well, Zach, you ready? There's three women here. The young ladies Ethel Lange, Nellie de Wet, and Betty Jones.

ZACHARIAH. So what do we do?

MORRIS. I'll get the ball rolling with this thought. They are all pretty good names. Ethel, Nellie, and Betty. Good, simple, decent, common names. About equal, I'd say.

ZACHARIAH [*hopefully*]. There's no Connie there, is there Morrie?

MORRIS. No. Now, before you decide, let me tell you about them.

ZACHARIAH. What do you know about them?

MORRIS. It's written down here. That's why you bought the paper. Listen . . . [*Reads.*] 'Ethel Lange, 10 de Villiers Street, Oudtshoorn. I am eighteen years old and well-developed and would like to correspond with a gent of sober habits and a good outlook on life. My interests are nature, rock-and-roll, swimming, and a happy future. My motto is, "Rolling stones gather no moss." Please note: I promise to reply faithfully.' How's that?

ZACHARIAH. Well-developed.

MORRIS. She gives you a clear picture, hey! Here's the next one. [*Reads.*] 'Nellie de Wet' . . . she's in Bloemfontein . . . 'Twenty-two and no strings attached. Would like letters from men of the same age or older. My interests are beauty contests and going out. A snap with the first letter, please.' [*Pause.*] That's all there is to her. I think I preferred Ethel.

ZACHARIAH. *Ja.* And what do I know how old I am?

MORRIS. Exactly, Zach! 'The same age or older?' Where does she think she comes from?

ZACHARIAH. Bloemfontein.

MORRIS. Yes. Last one. [*Reads.*] 'Betty Jones. Roodepoort.

Young and pleasing personality. I'd like to correspond with gentlemen friends of maturity. No teenagers need reply. My hobby at the moment is historical films, but I'm prepared to go back to last year's, which was autograph hunting. I would appreciate a photograph.' That one's got a education. Anyway . . . it's up to you. Ethel, Nellie, or Betty?

ZACHARIAH [*after thinking about it*]. Hey, hey, Morrie! Let's take all three.

MORRIS. No, Zach.

ZACHARIAH. *Ag*, come on, man.

MORRIS. You don't understand.

ZACHARIAH. Just once, just for sports.

MORRIS. I don't think they'd allow that.

ZACHARIAH. Oh.

MORRIS. No, they wouldn't.

  [*Pause, emphatic.*]

Listen, Zach, you must take this serious.

ZACHARIAH. Okay.

MORRIS [*losing patience*]. Well, it's no good saying 'Okay' like that!

ZACHARIAH. Okay!

MORRIS. What's the use, Zach? You ask me to help you, and when I do, you're not interested no more. What's the matter, man?

ZACHARIAH. I can't get hot about a name on a piece of paper. It's not real to me.

MORRIS [*outraged*]. Not real! [*Reads.*] 'I am eighteen years old and well-developed' . . . eighteen years old and well-developed! If I called that Connie it would be real enough, wouldn't it?

ZACHARIAH [*his face lighting up*]. *Ja!*

MORRIS. So the only difference is a name. This is Ethel and not Connie . . . which makes no difference to being eighteen years old and well-developed! Think, man!

ZACHARIAH. [*Without hesitation.*] Look, Morrie, I'll take her.

MORRIS. That's better. So it's going to be Miss Ethel Lange

from Oudtshoorn, who would like to correspond with a gent of sober habits and a good outlook on life. [*Putting down the paper.*] Yes, she's the one for you all right. And I know what we do. How about asking Ethel to take a snapshot of herself? So we can see what her outlook is. Then—just think of it—you can see her, hear from her, write to her, correspond with her, post your letter off to her . . . Hell, man! What more do you want! [*Zachariah smiles.*] No! That's something else. This is pen-pals, and you got yourself Ethel in Oudtshoorn.

[*Morris moves to the table where he sorts out a piece of writing-paper, a pencil, and an envelope.*]

I've got everything ready. One day I must show you how. Maybe have a go at a letter yourself. Address in the top right-hand corner. Mr Zachariah Pietersen, Korsten, P. O. Port Elizabeth. Okay, now take aim and fire away. [*He waits for Zachariah.*] Well?

ZACHARIAH. What?

MORRIS. Speak to Ethel.

ZACHARIAH [*shy*]. Go jump in a lake, man.

MORRIS. No, listen, Zach. I'm sitting here ready to write. You must speak up.

ZACHARIAH. What?

MORRIS. To begin with, address her.

ZACHARIAH. What?

MORRIS. Address her.

ZACHARIAH. Oudtshoorn.

MORRIS. No, no, Zach. Look, imagine there was a woman, and you want to say something to her, what would you say? Go on.

ZACHARIAH. Hey! Cookie . . . or . . . *Bokkie* . . .

MORRIS [*quickly*]. Okay, Zach . . . You're getting hot, but that is what we call a personal address, you only use it later. This time you say: 'Dear Ethel'.

ZACHARIAH. Just like that?

MORRIS. You get her on friendly terms. Now comes the introduction. [*Writes.*] 'With reply to your advert for a pen-pal, I hereby write.' [*Holds up the writing paper.*] Now tell her who you are and where you are.

ZACHARIAH. How?

MORRIS. I am . . . and so on.

ZACHARIAH. I am Zach and I . . .

MORRIS. . . . ariah Pietersen . . .

ZACHARIAH. And I am at Korsten.

MORRIS. 'As you will see from the above.'

ZACHARIAH. What's that?

MORRIS. Something you must always add in letters, Zach. [*Newspaper.*] Now she says here: 'My interests are nature, rock-and-roll, swimming, and a happy future.' Well, what do you say to that?

ZACHARIAH. Shit! [*Pause, frozen stare from Morris.*] Oh, sorry, Morrie, sorry. 'Nature and a happy future.' *Ja.* Well, good luck! Good luck, Ethel. How's that?

MORRIS. Not bad. A little short, though. How about: I notice your plans, and wish you good luck with them.

ZACHARIAH. Sure, sure. Put that there.

MORRIS [*writes, then returns to the newspaper*]. '. . . plans, and wish you good luck with them.' Okay, next—'My motto is: "Rolling stones gather no moss".' [*Pause.*] That's tricky.

ZACHARIAH. *Ja*, I can see that.

MORRIS. What does she mean?

ZACHARIAH. I wonder.

MORRIS. Wait! I think I've got it. How about: 'Too many cooks spoil the broth'? That's my favourite.

ZACHARIAH. Why not? Why not, I ask?

MORRIS. Then it's agreed. [*Writes.*] 'Experience has taught me to make my motto: "Too many cooks spoil the broth".' Now let's get a little bit general, Zach.

ZACHARIAH [*yawning*]. Just as you say.

MORRIS [*after a pause*]. Well, it's your letter.

ZACHARIAH. Just a little bit general. Not too much, hey?

MORRIS [*not fooled by the feigned interest. Pause*]. I can make a suggestion.

ZACHARIAH. That's fine. Put that down there, too.

MORRIS. No, Zach. Here it is. How about: 'I have a brother who has seen Oudtshoorn twice.'

ZACHARIAH. You.

MORRIS. Yes.

ZACHARIAH. Maybe.

MORRIS. You mean you don't like it?

ZACHARIAH. Tell you what. Put down there: 'I'd like to see Oudtshoorn. I've heard about it from . . . someone. I'd like to see you, too. Send me a photo.'

MORRIS. '. . . please' . . . I'm near the bottom now.

ZACHARIAH. That's all.

MORRIS. 'Please write soon. Yours . . .'

ZACHARIAH. Hers?

MORRIS. '. . . faithfully. Zachariah Pietersen.'

[*Zachariah prepares for bed. Morris addresses and seals the envelope.*]

I'll get this off tomorrow. Now remember, this is your letter, and what comes back is going to be your reply.

ZACHARIAH. And yours?

MORRIS. Mine?

ZACHARIAH. There's still Nellie or Betty. Plenty of big words there, as I remember.

MORRIS. One's enough, Zach. [*Alarm-clock rings.*] Bed time. [*Takes down his Bible.*] My turn to choose the reading tonight, Zach. [*Chooses a passage.*] Matthew. I like Matthew. [*Reads.*] 'And Asa begat Josaphat, and Josaphat begat Joram, and Joram begat Ozias; and Ozias begat Joatham, and Joatham begat Achaz, and Achaz begat Ezekias; and Ezekias begat Manassas, and Manassas begat Amon, and Amon begat . . .' [*Pause.*] That must have been a family. [*Puts away the Bible and prepares his own bed.*] Why you looking at me like that, Zach?

ZACHARIAH. I'm thinking.

MORRIS. Out with it. Let's hear!

ZACHARIAH. You ever had a woman, Morris?

[*Morris looks at Zachariah blankly, then pretends he hasn't heard.*]

MORRIS. What do you mean?

ZACHARIAH. Come on, you know what I mean.

MORRIS. Why?

ZACHARIAH. Have—you—ever—had—woman? Why have I never thought of that before? You been here a long time now, and never once did you go out, or speak to me about woman. Not like Minnie. Anything the matter with you?

MORRIS. Not like Minnie! What's that mean? Not like Minnie! Maybe it's not nice to be like Minnie. Or maybe I just don't want to be like Minnie! Ever thought about that? That there might be another way, a different way? Listen. You think I don't know there's women in this world, that I haven't got two legs and trousers too? That I haven't longed for beauty? Well, I do. But that's not what you're talking about, is it? That's not what Minnie means, hey! That's two bloody donkeys on a road full of stones and Connie crying in the bushes. Well, you're right about that, Zach. I am not interested. I touched something else once, with my life and these hands . . . just touched it and felt warmth and softness and wanted it like I've never wanted anything in my whole life. Ask me why I didn't take it when I touched it. That's the question. Do you want to know why, Zach? Do you? Zach? [*Pause, then softly.*] Zachariah?

[*Zachariah is asleep. Morris covers him with a blanket.*]

SCENE THREE

A few days later.

Morris is at the table counting their savings—banknotes and silver. The alarm-clock rings. He sweeps the money into a tin which he then carefully hides among the pots on the kitchen-dresser. Next he resets the clock and prepares the footbath as in the first scene. Zachariah appears, silent and sullen, goes straight to the bed, where he sits.

MORRIS. You look tired tonight, old fellow.

[*Zachariah looks at him askance.*]

Today too long?

ZACHARIAH. What's this 'old fellow' thing you got hold of tonight?

MORRIS. Just a figure of speaking, Zach. The Englishman would say 'old boy' . . . but we don't like that 'boy' business, hey?

ZACHARIAH. *Ja.* They call a man a boy. You got a word for that, Morrie?

MORRIS. Long or short?

ZACHARIAH. Squashed, like it didn't fit the mouth.

MORRIS. I know the one you mean.

ZACHARIAH. *Ja*, then say it.

MORRIS. Prejudice.

ZACHARIAH. Pre-ja-dis.

MORRIS. Injustice!

ZACHARIAH. That's all out of shape as well.

MORRIS. Inhumanity!

ZACHARIAH. No. That's when he makes me stand at the gate.

MORRIS. Am I right in thinking you were there again today?

ZACHARIAH. All day long.

MORRIS. You tried to go back to pots?

ZACHARIAH. I tried to go back to pots. 'My feet', I said, 'are killing me.'

MORRIS. And then?

ZACHARIAH. He said, 'Go to the gate or go to hell . . . Boy!'

MORRIS. He said 'boy' as well?

ZACHARIAH. He did.

MORRIS. In one sentence?

ZACHARIAH. Prejudice and inhumanity in one sentence!

[*He starts to work off one shoe with the other foot and then dips the bare foot into the basin of water. He will not get as far as taking off the other shoe.*]

When your feet are bad, you feel it, man.

[*Morris starts helping Zachariah take off his coat. At this point Morris finds an envelope in the inside pocket of Zachariah's coat. He examines it secretly. Zachariah broods on, one foot in the basin.*]

MORRIS. Zach, did you stop by the Post Office on your way back?

ZACHARIAH. *Ja*. There was a letter there.

MORRIS. I know there was. [*Holding up the envelope.*] I just found it.

ZACHARIAH. Good.

MORRIS. What do you mean, 'good'?

ZACHARIAH. Good, like 'okay'.

MORRIS [*excited and annoyed*]. What's the matter with you?

ZACHARIAH. What's the matter with me?

MORRIS. This is your pen-pal. This is your reply from Ethel!

ZACHARIAH. In Oudtshoorn.

MORRIS. But Zach! You must get excited, man! Don't you want to know what she said?

ZACHARIAH. Sure.

MORRIS. Shall we open it then?

ZACHARIAH. Why not!

MORRIS [*tears open the letter*]. By God, she did it! She sent you a picture of herself.

ZACHARIAH [*first flicker of interest*]. She did?

MORRIS. So this is Ethel!

ZACHARIAH. Morrie . . . ?

MORRIS. Eighteen years . . . and fully . . . developed.

ZACHARIAH. Let me see, man!

25

[*He grabs the photograph. The certainty and excitement fade from Morris's face. He is obviously perplexed by something.*]

Hey! Not bad. Now that's what I call a goosie. Good for old Oudtshoorn. You don't get them like this over here. That I can tell you. Not with a watch! Pretty smart, too. Nice hair. Just look at those locks. And how's that for a wall she's standing against? Ever seen a wall like that, as big as that, in Korsten? I mean it's made of bricks, isn't it!

MORRIS [*snatching the photograph out of Zachariah's hand and taking it to the window where he has a good look*]. Zach, let me have another look at her.

ZACHARIAH. Hey! What's the matter with you! It's my pen-pal, isn't it? It is!

MORRIS. Keep quiet, Zach!

ZACHARIAH. What's this 'keep quiet'?

[*Morris throws the photograph down on the bed and finds the letter, which he reads feverishly. Zachariah picks up the photograph and continues his study.*]

ZACHARIAH. You're acting like you never seen a woman in your life. Why don't you get a pen-pal? Maybe one's not enough.

MORRIS [*having finished the letter, his agitation is now even more pronounced*]. That newspaper, Zach. Where is that newspaper?

ZACHARIAH. How should I know?

MORRIS [*anguished*]. Think, man!

ZACHARIAH. You had it. [*Morris is scratching around frantically.*] What's the matter with you tonight? Maybe you threw it away.

MORRIS. No. I was keeping it in case . . . [*Finds it.*] Thank God! Oh, please, God, now make it that I am wrong!

[*He takes a look at the newspaper, pages through it, and then drops it. He stands quite still, unnaturally calm after the frenzy of the previous few seconds.*]

You know what you done, don't you?

ZACHARIAH. Me?

MORRIS. Who was it, then? Me?

ZACHARIAH. But what?

MORRIS. Who wanted woman?

ZACHARIAH. Oh. Me.

MORRIS. Right. Who's been carrying on about Minnie, and Connie, and good times? Not me.

ZACHARIAH. Morrie! What are you talking about?

MORRIS. That photograph.

ZACHARIAH. I've seen it.

MORRIS. Have another look.

ZACHARIAH [*he does*]. It's Ethel.

MORRIS. Miss Ethel Lange to you!

ZACHARIAH. Okay, I looked. Now what!

MORRIS. Can't you see, man! Ethel Lange is a white woman!

[*Pause. They look at each other in silence.*]

ZACHARIAH [*slowly*]. You mean that this Ethel . . . here . . .

MORRIS. Is a white woman!

ZACHARIAH. How do you know?

MORRIS. Oh for God's sake, Zach—use your eyes. Anyway, that paper you bought was white. There's no news about our sort.

ZACHARIAH [*studying the photo*]. Hey—you're right, Morrie. [*Delighted.*] You're damn well right. And this white woman has written to me, a *hot-not*, a *swartgat*. This white woman thinks I'm a white man. That I like!

[*Zachariah bursts into laughter. Morris jumps forward and snatches the photograph out of his hand.*]

Hey! What are you going to do?

MORRIS. What do you think?

ZACHARIAH. Read it.

MORRIS. I'm going to burn it.

ZACHARIAH. No!

MORRIS. Yes.

ZACHARIAH [*jumps up and comes to grips with Morris who, after a short struggle, is thrown violently to the floor. Zachariah picks up the letter and the photograph. He stands looking down at Morris for a few seconds, amazed at what he has done*]. No, Morrie. You're not going to burn it, Morrie.

27

MORRIS [*vehemently*]. Yes, burn the bloody thing! Destroy it!

ZACHARIAH. But it's my pen-pal, Morris. Now, isn't it? Doesn't it say here: 'Mr Zachariah Pietersen'? Well, that's me . . . isn't it? It is. My letter. You just don't go and burn another man's letter, Morrie.

MORRIS. But it's an error, Zach! Can't you see? The whole thing is an error.

ZACHARIAH. Read the letter, man. I don't know.

[*The alarm-clock rings.*]

MORRIS. Supper time.

ZACHARIAH. Later.

MORRIS. Listen—

ZACHARIAH. Letter first.

MORRIS. Then can I burn it?

ZACHARIAH. Read the letter first, man. Let's hear it, what it says. [*Handing Morris the letter.*] No funny business, hey!

MORRIS [*reading*]. 'Dear Zach, many thanks for your letter You asked me for a snap, so I'm sending you it. Do you like it? That's my brother's foot sticking in the picture behind the bench on the side—'

ZACHARIAH. Hey! She's right! Here it is.

MORRIS. 'Cornelius is a . . . policeman.' [*Pause.*] 'He's got a motor-bike, and I been with him to the dam, on the back. My best friend is Lucy van Tonder. Both of us hates Oudtshoorn, man. How is Port Elizabeth? There's only two movies here, so we don't know what to do on the other nights. That's why I want pen-pals. How about a picture of you? You got a car? All for now. Cheerio. Ethel. P.S. Please write soon.'

(*Morris folds the letter.*)

ZACHARIAH [*gratefully*]. Oh—thank you, Morrie.

[*Holds out his hand for the letter.*]

MORRIS. Can I burn it now, Zach?

ZACHARIAH. Burn it! It's an all right letter, man. A little bit of this and a little bit of that.

MORRIS. Like her brother being a policeman.

ZACHARIAH [*ignoring the last remark*]. Hey—supper ready yet,

28

man? Let's talk after supper, man. I'm hungry. What you got for supper, Morrie?

MORRIS. Boiled eggs and chips.

ZACHARIAH. Hey, that's wonderful, Morrie. Hey! We never had that before.

MORRIS [*sulking*]. It was meant to be a surprise.

ZACHARIAH. But that's wonderful.

[*Zachariah is full of vigour and life.*]

No, I mean it, Morrie. Cross my heart, and hope to die. Boiled eggs and chips! Boiled eggs and chips . . . Boiled eggs and chips . . . I never even knew you could do it.

[*Zachariah takes his place at the table, and stands the photograph in front of him. When Morris brings the food to the table, he sees it and hesitates.*]

What's it got here on the back, Morrie?

MORRIS [*examines the back of the photograph*]. 'To Zach, with love, from Ethel.'

[*Another burst of laughter from Zachariah. Morris leaves the table abruptly.*]

ZACHARIAH [*calmly continuing with his meal*]. Hey—what's the matter?

MORRIS. I'm not hungry tonight.

ZACHARIAH. Oh, you mean, you don't like to hear me laugh?

MORRIS. It's not that . . . Zach.

ZACHARIAH. But it is. It's funny, man. She and me. Of course, it wouldn't be so funny if it was you who was pally with her.

MORRIS. What does that mean?

ZACHARIAH. Don't you know?

MORRIS. No. So will you please tell me?

ZACHARIAH. You never seen yourself, Morrie?

MORRIS [*trembling with emotion*]. I'm warning you Zach. Just be careful of where your words are taking you!

ZACHARIAH. Okay. Okay. Okay—

[*Eats in silence.*]

You was telling me about Oudtshoorn the other day. How far you say it was?

MORRIS [*viciously*]. Hundreds of miles.

ZACHARIAH. So far, hey?

MORRIS. Don't fool yourself, Zach. It's not far enough for safety's sake. Cornelius has got a motorbike, remember.

ZACHARIAH. *Ja*. But we don't write to him, man.

MORRIS. Listen. Zach, if you think for one moment that I'm going to write . . .

ZACHARIAH. Think? Think? Who says? I been eating my supper. It was good, Morrie. Boiled eggs and chips, tasty.

MORRIS. Don't try to change the subject-matter!

ZACHARIAH. Who? Me?

MORRIS. *Ja*—you.

ZACHARIAH. I like that. You mean, what's the matter with you? You was the one that spoke about pen-pals first. Not me.

MORRIS. So here it comes at last. I've been waiting for it. I'm to blame, am I? All right. I'll take the blame. I always did, didn't I? But this is where it ends. I'm telling you now, Zach, burn that letter, because when they come around here and ask me, I'll say I got nothing to do with it.

ZACHARIAH. Burn this letter! What's wrong with this letter?

MORRIS. Ethel Lange is a white woman!

ZACHARIAH. Wait . . . wait . . . not so fast, Morrie. I'm a sort of a slow man. We were talking about this letter, not her. Now tell me, what's wrong with what you did read? Does she call me names? No. Does she laugh at me? No. Does she swear at me? No. Just a simple letter with a little bit of this and a little bit of that. Here comes the clue. What sort of chap is it that throws away a few kind words? Hey, Morrie? Aren't they, as you say, precious things these days? And this pretty picture of a lovely girl? I burn it! What sort of doing is that? Bad. Think, man, think of Ethel, man. Think! Sitting up there in Oudtshoorn with Lucy, waiting . . . and waiting . . . and waiting . . . for what? For nothing. For why? Because bad Zach Pietersen burnt it. No, Morrie. Good is good, and fair is fair. I may be a shade of black, but I go gently as a man.

MORRIS [*pause*]. Are you finished now, Zach? Good, because I want to remind you, Zach, that when I was writing to her you weren't even interested in a single thing I said. But now, suddenly, now you are! Why? Why, I ask myself . . . and a suspicious little voice answers: is it maybe because she's white?

ZACHARIAH. You want to hear me say it?

[*Morris says nothing.*]

It's because she's white! I like this little white girl! I like the thought of this little white girl. I'm telling you I like the thought of this little white Ethel better than our plans, or future, or foot salts or any other damned thing in here. It's the best thought I ever had and I'm keeping it, and don't try no tricks like trying to get it away from me. Who knows? You might get to liking it too, Morrie.

[*Morris says nothing. Zachariah comes closer.*]

Ja. There's a thought there. What about you, Morrie? You never had it before—that thought? A man like you, specially you, always thinking so many things! A man like you who's been places! You're always telling me about the places you been. Wasn't there ever no white woman thereabouts? I mean . . . you must have smelt them someplace. That sweet, white smell, they leave it behind, you know. [*Nudging Morris.*] Come on, confess. Of course, you did. Hey? I bet you had that thought all the time. I bet you been having it in here. Hey? You should have shared it, Morrie. I'm a man with a taste for thoughts these days. It hurts to think you didn't share a good one like that with your brother. Giving me all the other shit about future and plans, and then keeping the real goosie for yourself. You weren't scared, were you? That I'd tell? Come on. Confess. You were. A little bit poopy. I've noticed that. But you needn't worry now. I'm a man for keeping a secret, and anyway, we'll play this very careful . . . very, very careful. Ethel won't never know about us, and I know how to handle that brother. Mustn't let a policeman bugger you about, man. So write. Write! We'll go gently with this one. There'll be others. Later.

[*Morris is defeated. He sits at the table. Zachariah fetches paper and pencil.*]

So we'll take her on friendly terms again. [*Pause.*] 'Dear Ethel,'

[*Morris writes.*] 'I think you'd like to know I got your letter, and the picture. I'd say Oudtshoorn seems okay. You were quite okay too. I would like to send you a picture of me, but it's this way. It's winter down here. The light is bad, the lake is black, the birds have gone. Wait for spring, when things improve. Okay? Good. I heard you ask about my car. Yes. I have it. We pumped the tyres today. And tomorrow I think I'll put in some petrol. I'd like to take you for a drive, Ethel, and Lucy too. In fact, I'd like to drive both of you. They say over here I'm fast. Ethel, I'll tell you this. If I could drive you, Ethel, and Lucy too, I'd do it so fast, fast, fast, fast, fast—'

MORRIS. Okay, Zach!

ZACHARIAH [*pulling himself together*]. '*Ja*! But don't worry. I got brakes.' [*Pause.*] 'I notice your brother got boots. All policemen got boots. Good luck to him, anyway, and Lucy too. Write soon. Zachariah Pietersen.' [*Pause.*] Okay, Morrie. There, you see! Just a simple letter with a little bit of this and a little bit of that and nothing about some things. When Ethel gets it she'll say: 'He's okay. This Zachariah Pietersen is okay, Lucy!' Oh, say something, Morrie.

MORRIS. Zach, please listen to me. [*Pause.*] Let me burn it.

ZACHARIAH. My letter?

MORRIS. Yes.

ZACHARIAH. The one we just done?

MORRIS. Yes.

ZACHARIAH. Ethel's letter, now my letter!

[*He gets up and takes the letter in question away from Morris.*]
You're in a burning mood tonight, Morrie.

MORRIS. Please, Zach. You're going to get hurt.

ZACHARIAH [*aggression*]. Such as by who?

MORRIS. Ethel. Then yourself.

[*Zachariah laughs.*]
Oh yes. That. There in your hand. To Miss Ethel Lange. Oudtshoorn. You think that's a letter? I'm telling you it's a dream, and the most dangerous one. And now you have it on paper as well. That's what they call evidence, you know. [*Pause.*] Shit, Zach, I have a feeling about this business, man!

ZACHARIAH. Oh come on, cheer up, Morrie. It's not so bad.

MORRIS. But you're playing with fire, Zach.

ZACHARIAH. Maybe. But then I never had much to play with.

MORRIS. Didn't you?

ZACHARIAH. Don't you remember? You got the toys.

MORRIS. Did I?

ZACHARIAH. *Ja*. Like that top, Morrie. I have always remembered that brown stinkwood top. She gave me her old cotton-reels to play with, but it wasn't the same. I wanted a top.

MORRIS. Who? Who gave me the top?

ZACHARIAH. Mother.

MORRIS. Mother!

ZACHARIAH. *Ja*. She said she only had one. There was always only one.

MORRIS. Zach, you're telling me a thing now!

ZACHARIAH. What? Did you forget her?

MORRIS. No, Zach. I meant the top. I can't remember that top. And what about her, Zach? There's a memory for you. I tried it out the other night. 'Mother', I said, 'Mother'! A sadness, I thought.

ZACHARIAH. *Ja*.

MORRIS. Just a touch of sadness.

ZACHARIAH. A soft touch with sadness.

MORRIS. And soapsuds on brown hands.

ZACHARIAH. And sore feet.

[*Pause. Morris looks at Zachariah.*]

MORRIS. What do you mean?

ZACHARIAH. There was her feet, man.

MORRIS. Who had feet?

ZACHARIAH. Mother, man.

MORRIS. I don't remember her feet, Zach.

ZACHARIAH [*serenely confident*]. There was her feet, man. The toes were crooked, the nails skew, and there was pain. They didn't fit the shoes.

MORRIS [*growing agitation*]. Zach, are you sure that wasn't somebody else?

33

ZACHARIAH. It was mother's feet. She let me feel the hardness and then pruned them down with a razor blade.

MORRIS. No, Zach. You got me worried now! A grey dress?

ZACHARIAH. Maybe.

MORRIS [*persistent*]. Going to church, remember? She wore it going to—

ZACHARIAH. The butcher shop! That's it! That's where she went.

MORRIS. What for?

ZACHARIAH. For tripe.

MORRIS. Tripe? Stop, Zach. Stop! This is beginning to sound like some other mother.

ZACHARIAH [*gently*]. How can that be?

MORRIS. Listen, Zach. Do you remember the songs she sang?

ZACHARIAH. Do I! [*He laughs and then sings:*]

> 'My skin is black
> The soap is blue,
> But the washing comes out white.
>
> I took a man
> On a Friday night;
> Now I'm washing a baby too.
>
> Just a little bit black,
> And a little bit white,
> He's a Capie through and through.'

[*Morris is staring at him in horror.*]

MORRIS. That wasn't what she sang to me. 'Lullabye baby', it was, 'You'll get to the top.' [*Anguish.*] This is some sort of terrible error. Wait . . . wait! I've got it . . . Oh, God, please let it be that I've got it! [*To Zachariah.*] How about the games we played? Think, Zach. Think carefully! There was one special one. Just me and you. I'll give you a clue. Toot-toot. Toot-toot.

ZACHARIAH [*thinking*]. Wasn't there an old car?

MORRIS. Where would it be?

ZACHARIAH. Rusting by the side of the road.

MORRIS. Could it be the ruins of an old Chevy, Zach?

ZACHARIAH. Yes, it could.

MORRIS. And can we say without tyres and wires and things?

ZACHARIAH. We may.

MORRIS. . . . and all the glass blown away by the wind?

ZACHARIAH. Dusty.

MORRIS. Deserted.

ZACHARIAH. Sting bees on the bonnet.

MORRIS. Webs in the windscreen.

ZACHARIAH. Nothing in the boot.

MORRIS. And us?

ZACHARIAH. In it.

MORRIS. We are? How?

ZACHARIAH. Side by side.

MORRIS. Like this?

[*He sits beside Zachariah.*]

ZACHARIAH. Uh-huh.

MORRIS. Doing what?

ZACHARIAH. Staring.

MORRIS. Not both of us!

ZACHARIAH. Me at the wheel, you at the window.

MORRIS. Okay. Now what?

ZACHARIAH. Now, I got this gear here and I'm going to go.

MORRIS. Where?

ZACHARIAH. To hell and gone, and we aren't coming back.

MORRIS. What will I do while you drive?

ZACHARIAH. You must tell me what we pass. Are you ready? Here we go!

[*Zachariah goes through the motion of driving a car. Morris looks eagerly out of the window.*]

MORRIS. We're slipping through the streets, passing houses and people on the pavements who are quite friendly and wave as we drive by. It's a fine, sunny sort of a day. What are we doing?

ZACHARIAH. Twenty-four.

MORRIS. Do you see that bus ahead of us?

35

[*They lean over to one side as Zachariah swings the wheel. Morris looks back.*]

Chock-a-block with early morning workers. Shame. And what about those children over there, going to school? Shame again. On such a nice day. What are we doing?

ZACHARIAH. Thirty-four.

MORRIS. That means we're coming to open country. The houses have given way to patches of green and animals and not so many people anymore. But they still wave . . . with their spades.

ZACHARIAH. Fifty.

MORRIS. You're going quite fast. You've killed a cat, flattened a frog, frightened a dog . . . who jumped!

ZACHARIAH. Sixty.

MORRIS. Passing trees, and haystacks, and sunshine, and the smoke from little houses drifting up . . . shooting by!

ZACHARIAH. Eighty!

MORRIS. Birds flying abreast, and bulls, billygoats, black sheep . . .

ZACHARIAH. One hundred!

MORRIS. . . . cross a river, up a hill, to the top, coming down, down, down . . . stop! Stop!

ZACHARIAH [*slamming on the brakes*]. Eeeeeoooooooaah! [*Pause.*] Why?

MORRIS. Look! There's a butterfly.

ZACHARIAH. On your side?

MORRIS. Yours as well. Just look.

ZACHARIAH. All around us, hey!

MORRIS. This is rare, Zach! We've driven into a flock of butterflies.

ZACHARIAH. Butterflies! [*Smiles and then laughs.*]

MORRIS. We've found it, Zach. We've found it! This is our youth!

ZACHARIAH. And driving to hell and gone was our game.

MORRIS. Our best one! Hell, Zach, the things a man can forget!

ZACHARIAH. *Ja*, those were the days.

36

MORRIS. God knows.

ZACHARIAH. Goodness, hey!

MORRIS. They were that.

ZACHARIAH. And gladness too.

MORRIS. Making hay, man, come and play, man, while the sun is shining . . . which it did.

ZACHARIAH. Hey—what's that . . . that *nice* thing you say, Morrie?

MORRIS 'So sweet—

ZACHARIAH. Uh-huh.

MORRIS. '—did pass that summertime
Of youth and fruit upon the tree
When laughing boys and pretty girls
Did hop and skip and all were free.'

ZACHARIAH. Did *skop* and skip the pretty girls.

MORRIS. Hopscotch.

ZACHARIAH. That was it.

MORRIS We played our games, Zach.

ZACHARIAH. And now?

MORRIS. See for yourself, Zach. Here we are, later, and now there is Ethel as well and that makes me frightened.

ZACHARIAH. Sounds like another game.

MORRIS. Yes . . . but not ours this time. Hell, man, I often wonder.

ZACHARIAH. Same here.

MORRIS. I mean, where do they go, the good times, in a man's life?

ZACHARIAH. And the bad ones?

MORRIS. That's a thought. Where do *they* come from?

ZACHARIAH. Oudtshoorn.

SCENE FOUR

An evening later.

Zachariah is seated at the table, eating. He is obviously in good spirits, radiating inward satisfaction and secrecy. Morris moves about nervously behind his back.

MORRIS. So, it has come to this. Who would have thought it, hey! That one day, one of us would come in here with a secret and keep it to himself! If someone had told me that, I would have thrown up my hands in horror. To Morrie and Zach! . . . I would have cried. No! Emphatically not! [*Pause.*] It just goes to show you. Because I was wrong, wasn't I? There is a secret in this room, at this very moment. This is how brotherhood gets wrecked, you know, Zach, in secrecy. It's the hidden things that hurt and do the harm. [*Pause. Morris watches Zachariah's back.*] So, do you want to tell me?

ZACHARIAH. What are you talking about, Morrie?

MORRIS. You got a letter today, didn't you?

ZACHARIAH. Who?

MORRIS. You.

ZACHARIAH. What?

MORRIS. A letter. From Ethel. And you're not telling me about it. [*Zachariah continues eating, unaffected by Morris's words.*] Okay. Same sort as usual? [*Zachariah looks at Morris.*] The letter. [*Zachariah puts down his bread and thinks. Morris seizes his opportunity.*] Didn't you notice? Hell, Zach! You surprise me.

ZACHARIAH. No, what do you mean: the same sort?

MORRIS. Zach?

ZACHARIAH. So I'm asking you—what do you mean?

MORRIS. To begin with, there's the . . . envelope. Is it the same colour, or isn't it? I can see somebody didn't take a good look, did he?

[*Reluctantly, Zachariah takes the letter out of his inside pocket.*]
She's changed her colours! They used to be blue, remember? What about inside?

ZACHARIAH. I'm not ready for that yet.,

MORRIS. Okay. All I'm saying is . . . I don't care.

38

ZACHARIAH [*studying the envelope*]. I see they got animals on stamps nowadays. Donkeys with stripes.

MORRIS. Zebras.

ZACHARIAH. *Ja* . . . with stripes.

MORRIS. That's not the point about a letter, Zach.

ZACHARIAH. What?

MORRIS. The stamps. You're wasting your time with the stamps, man. It's what's inside that you got to read.

ZACHARIAH. You're in a hurry, Morrie.

MORRIS. Who?

ZACHARIAH. You.

MORRIS. Look, I told you before, all I'm saying is . . . I don't care and those stamps don't count.

ZACHARIAH. And my name on the envelope. How do you like that, hey?

MORRIS. Your name?

ZACHARIAH. *Ja*. My name.

MORRIS. Oh.

ZACHARIAH. Now what do you mean, with an 'Oh' like that?

MORRIS. What makes you so sure that that is your name? [*Zachariah is trapped.*] How do you spell your name, Zach? Come on, let's hear.

ZACHARIAH [*after a long struggle*]. Zach . . . ar . . . ri . . . yah.

MORRIS. Oh, no, you don't! That's no spelling. That's a pronounciation. A b c d and e . . . that's the alphabet.

[*After a moment's hesitation, Zachariah holds up the letter so that Morris can see the address.*]

ZACHARIAH. Is it for me, Morrie?

MORRIS. I'm not sure.

ZACHARIAH. Zachariah Pietersen.

MORRIS. I know your name. It's for one Z. Pietersen.

ZACHARIAH. Well, that's okay then.

MORRIS. Is it?

ZACHARIAH. Isn't it?

MORRIS. Since when are you the only thing around here that

begins with a Z? And how many Pietersens didn't we know as boys right here in this very selfsame Korsten?

ZACHARIAH [*keeps the letter for a few more seconds, then hands it to Morris*]. You win. Read it.

MORRIS I win! Good old Zach. [*Laughs happily, nudging Zachariah.*] It pays to have a brother who can read, hey? [*Opens the letter.*] Okay, Zach. 'Dear Zach, How's things? I'm okay, today, again. I got your letter ... Lucy had a laugh at you ...'

ZACHARIAH. What's funny?

MORRIS. I don't think she means that sort of laugh, Zach. I'm sure she means the friendly sort. [*Continues reading.*] 'Lucy had a laugh at you, but my brother is not so sure.' [*Pause.*] That, I feel, means something, Zach. What does it do to you?

ZACHARIAH. Nothing.

MORRIS. Remember his boots.

ZACHARIAH. No, nothing.

MORRIS [*reads on*]. 'I'm looking forward to a ride in your car ...' Zach, they believed it. [*Zachariah smiles.*] They believed our cock-and-bull about the car.

ZACHARIAH. [*Laughing.*] I told you.

MORRIS. 'I'm looking forward to a ride in your car ... and what about Lucy? Can she come?'

[*Their amusement knows no bounds.*]

ZACHARIAH. You must come too, Morrie. You and Lucy! Hey! We'll take them at ninety.

MORRIS. To hell and gone! [*Reads on through his laughter.*] Okay, Zach. 'We're coming down for a holiday in June, so where ... can we ... meet you?' [*Long pause. He reads again.*] 'We're coming down for a holiday in June, so where can we meet you?'

ZACHARIAH. Ethel ...?

MORRIS. Is coming here.

ZACHARIAH. Coming here?

MORRIS [*puts down the letter and stands up*]. I warned you, didn't I? I said: I have a feeling about this business. I remember my words. And wise ones they turned out to be. I told you to leave it alone. Hands off! I said. Don't touch! Not for you! But oh no, Mr Z. Pietersen was clever. He knew how to handle it. Well, handle this, will you please?

ZACHARIAH [*dumbly*]. What else does she say?

MORRIS [*brutally*]. I'm not going to read it. You want to know why? Because it doesn't matter. The game's up, man. Nothing matters except: 'I'm coming down in June, so where can I meet you?' That is what Mr Z. Pietersen had better start thinking about . . . and quick, boy, quick!

ZACHARIAH. When's June?

MORRIS. Soon.

ZACHARIAH. How soon?

MORRIS [*ticking them off on his fingers*]. June, July, August, September, October, November, December, January, February, March, April, May, June. Satisfied?

[*Another long pause.*]

ZACHARIAH. So?

MORRIS [*to the table, where he reads further into the letter*]. I'll be staying with my uncle at Kensington.' [*Little laugh.*] Kensington! Near enough for you, Zach? About five minutes walking from here, hey?

ZACHARIAH [*frightened*]. Morrie, I know. I'll tell her I can't see her.

MORRIS. She'll want to know why.

ZACHARIAH. Because I'm sick, with my heart.

MORRIS. And if she feels sorry and comes to comfort you?

ZACHARIAH [*growing desperation*]. No, but I'm going away.

MORRIS. When?

ZACHARIAH. Soon, soon. June. June! Morrie, June!

MORRIS. And what about where, and why and what, if she says she'll wait until you come back?

ZACHARIAH. Then I'll tell her . . .

[*Pause. He can think of nothing else to say.*]

MORRIS. What? You can't even tell her you're dead. You see, I happen to know. There is no white-washing away a man's facts. They'll speak for themselves at first sight, if you don't say it.

ZACHARIAH. Say what?

MORRIS. The truth. You know it.

ZACHARIAH. I don't. I know nothing.

MORRIS. Then listen, Zach, because I know it. 'Dear Ethel, forgive me, but I was born a dark sort of boy who wanted to play with whiteness . . .'

ZACHARIAH [*rebelling*]. No!

MORRIS. What else can you say? Come on. Let's hear it. What is there a man can say or pray that will change the colour of his skin or blind them to it?

ZACHARIAH. There must be something.

MORRIS. There's nothing . . . when it's a question of smiles and whispers and thoughts in strange eyes there is only the truth and . . . then . . . [*He pauses.*]

ZACHARIAH. And then what?

MORRIS. And then to make a run for it. They don't like these games with their whiteness, Zach. Ethel's got a policeman brother, remember, and an uncle and your address.

ZACHARIAH. What have I done, hey? I done nothing.

MORRIS. What have you thought, Zach! That's the crime. I seem to remember somebody saying: 'I like the thought of this little white girl.' And what about your dreams, Zach? They've kept me awake these past few nights. I've heard them mumbling and moaning away in the darkness. They'll hear them quick enough. When they get their hands on a dark-born boy playing with a white idea, you think they don't find out what he's been dreaming at night? They've got ways and means, Zach. Mean ways. Like confinement, in a cell, on bread and water, for days without end. They got time. All they need for evidence is a man's dreams. Not so much his hate. They say they can live with that. It's his dreams that they drag off to judgement. [*Pause. Goes back to the window. Turns to Zachariah.*] What are you going to do, Zach?

ZACHARIAH. I'm thinking about it, Morrie.

MORRIS. What are you thinking about it?

ZACHARIAH. What am I going to do?

MORRIS. You'd better be quick, man.

ZACHARIAH. Help me, Morrie.

MORRIS. Are you serious?

ZACHARIAH. I'm not smiling.

MORRIS. Okay, let's begin at the beginning, Zach. Give me the first fact.

ZACHARIAH [*severe and bitter*]. Ethel is white, and I am black.

MORRIS. That's a very good beginning, Zach.

ZACHARIAH. If she sees me . . .

MORRIS. Keep it up.

ZACHARIAH. . . . she'll be surprised.

MORRIS. Harder, Zach.

ZACHARIAH. She'll laugh.

MORRIS. Let it hurt, man!

ZACHARIAH. She'll scream!

MORRIS. Good! Now for yourself. She's surprised, remember?

ZACHARIAH. I'm not strange.

MORRIS. She swears?

ZACHARIAH. I'm no dog.

MORRIS. She screams!

ZACHARIAH. I just wanted to smell you, lady!

MORRIS. Good, Zach. Very good. You're seeing this clearly, man. But, remember there is still the others.

ZACHARIAH. What others?

MORRIS. The uncles with fists and brothers in boots who come running when a lady screams. What about them?

ZACHARIAH. What about them?

MORRIS. They've come to ransack you.

ZACHARIAH. I'll say it wasn't me.

MORRIS. They won't believe you.

ZACHARIAH. Leave me alone!

MORRIS. They'll hit you for that.

ZACHARIAH. I'll fight.

MORRIS. Too many for you.

ZACHARIAH. I'll call a policeman.

MORRIS. He's on their side.

ZACHARIAH. I'll run away!

MORRIS. That's better. Go back to the beginning. Give me that first fact, again. [*Pause.*] It started with Ethel, remember Ethel . . . is

ZACHARIAH. . . . is white.

MORRIS. That's it. And . . .

ZACHARIAH. . . . and I am black.

MORRIS. Let's hear it.

ZACHARIAH. Ethel is so . . . so . . . snow white.

MORRIS. And . . . come on . . .

ZACHARIAH. And I am too . . . truly . . . too black.

MORRIS. Now, this is the hard part, Zach. So let it hurt, man. It has to hurt a man to do him good. I know, just this one cry and then never again . . . Come one, Zach . . . let's hear it.

ZACHARIAH. I can never have her.

MORRIS. Never ever.

ZACHARIAH. She wouldn't want me anyway.

MORRIS. It's as simple as that.

ZACHARIAH. She's too white to want me anyway.

MORRIS. For better or for worse.

ZACHARIAH. So I won't want her anymore.

MORRIS. Not in this life, or that next one if death us do part, God help us! For ever and ever no more, thank you!

ZACHARIAH. The whole, rotten, stinking lot is all because I'm black! Black days, black ways, black things. They're me. I'm happy. Ha Ha Ha! Can you hear my black happiness? What is there is black as me?

MORRIS [*quietly, and with absolute sincerity*]. Oh, Zach! When I hear that certainty about whys and wherefores, about how to live and what not to love, I wish, believe me, man, I wish that old washerwoman had bruised me too at birth. I wish I was as—[*The alarm goes off.*] Bedtime.

[*Morris looks up to find Zachariah staring strangely at him. Morris goes to the window to avoid Zachariah's eyes. He turns from the window to find Zachariah still staring at him. Morris goes to the table to turn off the lamp.*]

ZACHARIAH. Morris!

MORRIS. Zach?

ZACHARIAH. Keep on the light.

MORRIS. Why?

ZACHARIAH. I saw something.

MORRIS. What?

ZACHARIAH. Your skin. How can I put it? It's . . . [*Pause.*]

MORRIS [*easily*]. On the light side.

ZACHARIAH. *Ja.*

MORRIS [*very easily*]. One of those things. [*Another move to the lamp.*]

ZACHARIAH. No, wait, wait, Morrie! I want to have a good look at you, man.

MORRIS. It's a bit late in the day to be seeing your brother for the first time. I been here a whole year, now, you know.

ZACHARIAH. *Ja.* But after a whole life I only seen myself properly tonight. You helped me. I'm grateful.

MORRIS. It was nothing,—Zach.

ZACHARIAH. No! I'm not a man that forgets a favour. I want to help you now.

MORRIS. I don't need any assistance, thank you, Zach.

ZACHARIAH. But you do. [*Morris sits.*] You're on the lighter side of life all right. You like that . . . all over? Your legs and things?

MORRIS. It's evenly spread.

ZACHARIAH. Not even a foot in the darker side, hey! I'd say you must be quite a bright boy with nothing on.

MORRIS. Please, Zach!

ZACHARIAH. You're shy! You always get undressed in the dark. Always well closed up. Like a woman. Like Ethel. I bet she shines. You know something? I bet if it was you she saw and not me she wouldn't say nothing.

[*Morris closes his eyes and gives a light, nervous laugh. Zachariah also laughs, but hollowly.*]

I'm sure she wouldn't be surprised, or laugh, or swear or scream. No one would come running. I bet all she would do is

45

say: 'How do you do, Mr Pietersen?' [*Pause.*] There's a thought there, Morrie. You ever think of it?

MORRIS. No.

ZACHARIAH. Not even a little bit of it? Like there, where you say: 'Hello, Ethel—' and shake hands. Ah, yes, I see this now. You would manage all right, Morrie. One thing is for certain: you would look all right, with her, and that's the main thing.

MORRIS. You're dreaming again, Zach.

ZACHARIAH. This is not my sort of dream. My dream was different. [*He laughs.*] I didn't shake her hands, Morrie. You're the man for shaking hands, Morrie.

MORRIS. Are you finished now, Zach?

ZACHARIAH. No. We're still coming to the big thought. Why don't you meet her? [*Pause.*]

MORRIS. You want to know why?

ZACHARIAH. *Ja.*

MORRIS. You really want to know?

ZACHARIAH. *Ja.*

MORRIS. She's not my pen-pal.

[*Morris moves to get away. Zachariah stops him.*]

ZACHARIAH. Okay, okay. Let's try it this way. Would you like to meet her?

MORRIS. Listen, Zach. I've told you before. Ethel is your—

ZACHARIAH [*pained*]. Please, Morrie! Would—you—like—to—meet—her?

MORRIS. That's no sort of question.

ZACHARIAH. Why not?

MORRIS. Because all my life I've been interested in meeting people. Not just Ethel—anybody!

ZACHARIAH. Okay, let's try it another way. Would you like to see her, or hear her, or maybe touch her?

MORRIS. That still doesn't give the question any meaning! You know me, Zach. Don't I like to hear church bells? Don't I like to touch horses? And anyway, I've told you before, Zach, Ethel is your pen-pal.

ZACHARIAH. You can have her.

46

MORRIS. What's this now?

ZACHARIAH. I'm giving her to you.

MORRIS [*angry*]. This is no bloody game, Zach!

ZACHARIAH. But I mean it. Look. I can't use her. We seen that. She'll see it too. But why throw away a good pen-pal if somebody else can do it? You can. Morrie, I'm telling you now, as your brother, that when Ethel sees you all she will do is say: 'How do you do, Mr Pietersen?' She'll never know otherwise.

MORRIS. You think so?

ZACHARIAH. You could fool me, if I didn't know who you were, Morrie.

MORRIS. You mean that, Zach?

ZACHARIAH. Cross my heart and hope to die. And the way you can talk! She'd be impressed, man.

MORRIS. That's true. I like to talk.

ZACHARIAH. No harm in it, is there? A couple of words, a little walk, and a packet of monkey-nuts.

MORRIS. Monkey-nuts?

ZACHARIAH. *Ja*. Something to chew.

MORRIS. Good God, Zach! You take a lady friend to tea, man!

ZACHARIAH. To tea, hey!

MORRIS. *Ja*, with buns, if she's hungry. Hot-cross buns.

ZACHARIAH. Now, you see! I would have just bought monkey-nuts. She's definitely not for me.

MORRIS. To tea. A pot of afternoon tea. When she wants to sit down, you pull out her chair . . . like this. [*He demonstrates*.]

ZACHARIAH. Hey—I think I seen that.

MORRIS. The woman pours the tea but the man butters the bun.

ZACHARIAH. Well, well, well.

MORRIS. Only two spoons of sugar, and don't drink out of the saucer.

ZACHARIAH. That's very good.

MORRIS. If she wants to blow her nose, offer your hanky, which you keep in your breast pocket.

47

ZACHARIAH. Go on.

MORRIS [*waking up to reality*]. You're wasting my time, Zach. I'm going to bed.

ZACHARIAH. But what's the matter, man? You been telling me everything so damn nice. Come on. Tell me. [*Coaxing.*] Tell your brother what's the matter.

MORRIS. I haven't got a hanky.

ZACHARIAH. I think we can buy one.

MORRIS. And the breast pocket?

ZACHARIAH. What's the problem there? Let's also—

MORRIS. Don't be a bloody fool! You got to buy a whole suit to get a breast pocket. And that's still not all. What about socks, decent shoes, a spotty tie, and a clean white shirt? How do you think a man steps out to meet a waiting lady. On his bare feet, wearing rags, and stinking because he hasn't had a bath? She'd even laugh and scream at me if I went like this. So I'm giving Ethel back to you. There is nothing I can do with her, thank you very much.

[*Morris crosses to his bed. Zachariah thinks.*]

ZACHARIAH. Haven't we got that sort of money?

MORRIS. All I got left until you get paid tomorrow is twenty cents. What the hell am I talking about! You know what a right sort of for-a-meeting-with-the-lady type of suit costs? Rands and rands and rands. Shoes? Rands and rands. Shirt? Rands. Then there's still two socks and a tie.

ZACHARIAH [*patiently*]. We got that sort of money.

MORRIS. Here you are. Twenty cents. Go buy me a suit.

ZACHARIAH. Thank you, Morrie. Where's the tin?

MORRIS. Tin?

ZACHARIAH. Square sort of tin.

MORRIS [*horror*]. You mean—our tin?

ZACHARIAH. There was sweets in it at Christmas.

MORRIS. Our future?

ZACHARIAH. That's the one. The future tin.

MORRIS. Our two-man farm?

ZACHARIAH. Yeah, where is it?

MORRIS. I won't tell you.

[*He runs and stands spread-eagled in front of the cupboard where the tin is hidden.*]

ZACHARIAH. Ah-ha!

MORRIS. No, Zach!

ZACHARIAH. Give it to me! Morrie!

MORRIS. No, Zach!—Zach, no . . .

[*Grabs the tin and runs away. Zachariah lurches after him. Morris is quick and elusive.*]

Zach, please! Just stop! Please! Just stand still and listen to me. Everything . . . everything we got, the most precious thing a man can have, a future, is in here. You've worked hard, I've done the saving.

ZACHARIAH. We'll start again.

MORRIS. It will take too long.

ZACHARIAH. I'll work overtime.

MORRIS. It won't be the same.

[*Zachariah lunges suddenly, but Morris escapes.*]

ZACHARIAH. Wait, Morrie! Wait! Fair is fair. Now this time you stand still . . . and listen.

MORRIS. I won't. I won't—no.

ZACHARIAH. Yes, you will, because Ethel is coming and you want to meet her. But like you say, not like any old *hotnot* in the street, but smartly. Now this is it. You're wearing a pretty-smart-for-a-meeting-with-the-lady type of suit.

[*Morris, clutching the tin to his chest, closes his eyes. Zachariah creeps closer.*]

Shiny shoes, white socks, a good shirt, and a spotty tie. And the people watch you go by and say: 'Hey! Who's you? There goes something!' And Ethel says: 'Who's this coming? Could it be my friend, Mr Pietersen?' And you say: 'Good day, Miss Ethel. Can I shake your white hands with my white hands?' 'Of course, Mr Pietersen.'

[*Zachariah has reached Morris. He takes the tin.*]

Thank you, Morrie.

[*Morris doesn't move. Zachariah opens the tin, takes out the money,*] *and then callously throws the tin away. He takes the money to the table where he counts it.*]

MORRIS. Why are you doing this to me?

ZACHARIAH. Aren't we brothers? [*Pause.*] What sort of suit? And what about the shoes?

MORRIS. Go to a good shop. Ask for the outfit, for a gentleman.

SCENE FIVE

The next day.
  Morris is lying on his bed, staring up at the ceiling. There is a knock at the door. Morris rises slowly on his bed.

MORRIS. Who's there? [*The knock is heard again.*] Speak up! I can't hear. [*Knocking.*] Who are you? [*Silence. Morris's fear is now apparent. He waits until the knock is heard a third time.*] Ethel . . . I mean, Madam . . . No! . . . I mean to say, Miss Ethel Lange, could that be you? [*In reply there is a raucous burst of laughter, unmistakably Zachariah's.*] What's this? [*Silence.*] What's the meaning of this? [*Morris rushes to his bed and looks at the alarm clock.*] It's still only the middle of the day.

ZACHARIAH. I know!

MORRIS. Go back to work! At once!

ZACHARIAH. I can't.

MORRIS. Why not?

ZACHARIAH. I took some leave, and left. Let me in, Morrie.

MORRIS. What's the matter with you? The door's not locked.

ZACHARIAH. My hands are full. [*Pause.*] I been shopping, Morrie.

  [*Morris rushes to the door, but collects himself before opening it. Zachariah comes in, his arms piled with parcels. He smiles slyly at Morris, who has assumed a pose of indifference.*]

Oh no you don't. I heard you run. So you thought it was our little Miss Ethel. And a little bit poopy at that thought. Well, don't worry, Morrie, 'cause you know what this is? Your outfit! Number one, and what do we have? A wonderful hat . . . sir.

  [*Takes it out and holds it up for approval. His manner is exaggerated, a caricature of the shopkeeper who sold him the clothing.*]

Which is guaranteed to protect the head on Sundays and rainy days. And next we have a good shirt and a grey tie, which is much better taste, because spots are too loud for a gentleman. Next we have—two grey socks, left and right, and a hanky to blow her nose. [*Next parcel.*] Aha! Now we've come to the suit. But before I show you the suit, my friend, I want to ask you, what does a man really look for in a good suit? A good cloth. Isn't that so?

MORRIS. What are you talking about?

ZACHARIAH. That's what he said. The fashion might be a season too old, but will you please feel the difference. It's lasted for years already. All what I can say is, take it or leave it. But only a fool would leave it at that price. So I took it. [*Next parcel.*] And next we have a real ostrich wallet.

MORRIS. What for?

ZACHARIAH. Your inside pocket. *Ja!* You forgot about the inside pocket. A gentleman always got a wallet for the inside pocket. [*Next parcel.*] And a cigarette case, and a cigarette lighter, for the outside pocket. Chramonium!

MORRIS. Since when do I smoke?

ZACHARIAH. I know, but Ethel might, he said.

MORRIS [*fear*]. You told him? Zach, are you out of your mind?

ZACHARIAH. Don't worry. I just said there was a lady who someone was going to meet. He winked at me and said it was a good thing, now and then, and reminded me that ladies like presents. [*Holds up a scarf.*] A pretty *doek* in case the wind blows her hair away. Ah-ha. And next we have an umbrella in case it's sopping wet. And over here . . . [*Last parcel.*] Guess what's in this box. I'll shake it. Listen.

MORRIS. Shoes.

ZACHARIAH [*triumphantly*]. No! It's boots! Ha, ha! *Ja.* [*Watching Morris's reaction.*] They frighten an *ou*, don't they? [*Happy.*] Satisfied, Morrie?

MORRIS [*looking at the pile of clothing*]. It seems all right

ZACHARIAH. It wasn't easy. At the first shop, when I asked for the outfit for a gentleman, they said I was an agitator, *ja*, and was going to call the police. I had to get out, man . . . quick! Even this fellow . . . Mr Moses . . . 'You're drunk,' he said. But when I showed him our future he sobered up. You know what he said? He said, 'Are you the gentleman?' So I said, 'Do I look like a gentleman, Mr Moses?' He said: 'My friend, it takes all sorts of different sorts to make this world.' 'I'm the black sort,' I said. So he said: 'You don't say.' He also said to mention his name to any other gentlemen wanting reasonable outfits. Go ahead, Morrie. [*The clothing.*] Let's see the gentle sort of man.

MORRIS. Okay. Okay. Don't rush me.

[*Moves cautiously to the pile of clothing. Flicks an imaginary speck of dust off the hat. Zachariah is waiting.*]

ZACHARIAH. Well?

MORRIS. Give me time.

ZACHARIAH. What for? You got the clothes, man.

MORRIS. For God's sake, Zach! This is deep water. I'm not just going to jump right in. You must paddle around first.

ZACHARIAH. Paddle around?

MORRIS. Try it out!

ZACHARIAH [*offering him the hat*]. No, try it on.

MORRIS. The idea, man. I got to try it out. There's more to wearing a white skin than just putting on a hat. You've seen white men before without hats, but they're still white men, aren't they?

ZACHARIAH. *Ja.*

MORRIS. And without suits or socks, or shoes . . .

ZACHARIAH. No, Morrie. Never without socks and shoes. Never a barefoot white man.

MORRIS. Well, the suit then. Look, Zach, what I'm trying to say is this. The clothes will help, but only help. They don't maketh the white man. It's that white something inside you, that special meaning and manner of whiteness. I know what I'm talking about because . . . I'll be honest with you now, Zach . . . I've thought about it for a long time. And the first fruit of my thought, Zach, is that this whiteness of theirs is not just in the skin, otherwise . . . well, I mean . . . I'd be one of them, wouldn't I? Because, let me tell you, Zach, I seen them that's darker than me.

ZACHARIAH. *Ja?*

MORRIS. Yes. Really dark, man. Only they had that something I'm telling you about . . . that's what I got to pin down in here.

ZACHARIAH. What?

MORRIS. White living, man! Like . . . like . . . like looking at things. Haven't you noticed it, Zach? They look at things

53

differently. Haven't you seen their eyes when they look at you? It's even in their way of walking.

ZACHARIAH. Ah—so you must learn to walk properly then.

MORRIS. Yes.

ZACHARIAH. And to look right at things.

MORRIS. *Ja.*

ZACHARIAH. And to sound right.

MORRIS. Yes! There's that, as well. The sound of it.

ZACHARIAH. So go on. [*Again offering the hat.*] Try it. For size. Just for the sake of the size.

[*Morris takes the hat, plays with it for a few seconds, then impulsively puts it on.*]

MORRIS. Just for size, okay.

ZACHARIAH. Ha!

MORRIS. Yes?

ZACHARIAH. Aha!

MORRIS [*whipping off the hat in embarrassment*]. No.

ZACHARIAH. Yes.

MORRIS [*shaking his head*]. Uhuh!

ZACHARIAH. Come.

MORRIS. No, man.

ZACHARIAH. Man. I like the look of that on your head.

MORRIS. It looked right?

ZACHARIAH. I'm telling you.

MORRIS. It seemed to fit.

ZACHARIAH. It did, I know.

MORRIS [*using this as an excuse to get it back on his head*]. The brim was just right on the brow . . . and with plenty of room for the brain! I'll try it again, shall I?

ZACHARIAH. Just for the sake of the size. A good fit.

MORRIS [*lifting the hat*]. Good morning!

ZACHARIAH. That's very good.

MORRIS [*again*]. Good morning . . . Miss Ethel Lange!

[*Looks quickly to see Zachariah's reaction. He betrays nothing.*]

ZACHARIAH. Maybe a little higher.

MORRIS. Higher? [*Again.*]

ZACHARIAH. *Ja.*

MORRIS. Good morning . . . [*A flourish.*] . . . and how do you do today, Miss Ethel Lange! [*Laughing with delight.*]

ZACHARIAH. How about the jacket?

MORRIS. Okay.

[*Zachariah hands him the jacket. He puts it on.*]

[*Preening.*] Zach—how did you do it?

ZACHARIAH. I said: 'The gentleman is smaller than me, Mr Moses.'

MORRIS [*once again lifting his hat*]. Good morning, Miss Ethel Lange . . . [*pleading, servile*]. I beg your pardon, but I do hope you wouldn't mind to take a little walk with . . .

ZACHARIAH. Stop!

MORRIS. What's wrong?

ZACHARIAH. Your voice.

MORRIS. What's wrong with it?

ZACHARIAH. Too soft. They don't ever sound like that.

MORRIS. To a lady they do! I admit, if it wasn't Ethel I was addressing it would be different.

ZACHARIAH. Okay. Try me.

MORRIS. You?

ZACHARIAH. You're walking with Ethel. I'm selling monkey-nuts.

MORRIS. So?

ZACHARIAH. So you want some monkey-nuts. Something to chew.

MORRIS. Ah! . . . [*His voice trails off.*]

ZACHARIAH. Go on. I'm selling monkey-nuts. Peanuts! Peanuts!

MORRIS [*after hesitation*]. I can't.

ZACHARIAH [*simulated shock*]. What!

MORRIS [*frightened*]. What I mean is . . . I don't want any monkey-nuts. I'm not hungry.

ZACHARIAH. Ethel wants some.

MORRIS. Ethel?

ZACHARIAH. *Ja*, and I'm selling them.

MORRIS. This is hard for me, Zach.

ZACHARIAH. You got to learn your lesson, Morrie. You want to pass, don't you? Peanuts! Peanuts!

MORRIS [*steeling himself*]. Excuse me!

ZACHARIAH. I'll never hear that. Peanuts!

MORRIS. Hey!

ZACHARIAH. Or that. Peanuts!

MORRIS. Boy!

ZACHARIAH. I'm ignoring you, man. I'm a cheeky one. Peanuts!

MORRIS. You're asking for it, Zach!

ZACHARIAH. I am.

MORRIS. I'm warning you. I will.

ZACHARIAH. Go on.

MORRIS [*with brutality and coarseness*]. Hey, *swartgat!*

[*An immediate reaction from Zachariah. His head whips round. He stares at Morris in disbelief. Morris replies with a weak little laugh, which soon dies on his lips.*]

Just a joke! [*Softly.*] I didn't mean it, Zach. Don't look at me like that! [*A step to Zachariah, who backs away.*] Say something. For God's sake, say anything! I'm your brother.

ZACHARIAH [*disbelief*]. My brother?

MORRIS. It's me, Zach, Morris!

ZACHARIAH. Morris?

MORRIS [*at last realizes what has happened. He tears off the jacket and | hat in a frenzy.*] Now do you see?

ZACHARIAH. That's funny. I thought . . . I was looking at a different sort of man.

MORRIS. But don't you see, Zach? It was me! That different sort of man you saw was me. It's happened, man. And I swear, I no longer wanted it. That's why I came back. Because . . . because . . . I'll tell you the whole truth now . . . because I did try it! It didn't seem a sin. If a man was born with a chance at changing why not take it? I thought . . . thinking of worms lying warm in their silk, to come out one day with wings and things! Why not a man? If his dreams are soft and keep him warm at night, why not stand up the next morning? Different . . . Beautiful! So what was stopping me? You. There was always you. What sort of thing was that to do to your own flesh and blood brother? Anywhere, any place or road, there was always you, Zach. So I came back. I'm no Judas. Gentle Jesus, I'm no Judas.

[*Pause. The alarm rings. Neither responds.*]

SCENE SIX

Night.

The two men are asleep. Silence. Suddenly Zachariah sits up in bed. Without looking at Morris he gets up, goes to the corner where the new suit of clothes is hanging, and puts on the suit and hat. The final effect is an absurdity bordering on the grotesque. The hat is too small and so is the jacket, which he has buttoned up incorrectly, while the trousers are too short. Zachariah stands barefooted, holding the umbrella, the hat pulled down low over his eyes so that his face is almost hidden.

ZACHARIAH. Ma. Ma. Ma! Mother! Hello. How are you, old woman? What's that? You don't recognize me? Well, well, well. Take a guess. Nope. Try again. Nope. [*Shakes his head.*] What's the matter with you, Ma? Don't you recognize your own son? [*Shakes his head violently.*] No, no, no, no! Not him! It's me, Zach! [*Sweeps off the hat to show his face.*] Ja. Zach! You didn't think I could do it, did you? Well, to tell you the truth, the whole truth so help me God, I got sick of myself and made a change. Him? At home, Ma. A lonely boy, as you say. A sad story, as I will tell you. He went on the road, Ma, but strange to say, he came back quite white. No tan at all. I don't recognize him no more. [*He sits.*] I'll ask you again, how are you, old woman? I see some signs of wear and tear. [*Nodding his head.*] That's true . . . such sorrow . . . tomorrow . . . *Ja* . . . it's cruel . . . your feet as well? Still a bad fit in the shoe? *Ai ai ai!* Me? [*Pause. He struggles.*] There's something I need to know, Ma. You see, I been talking, to him . . . *ja*, I talk to him, he says it helps . . . and now we got to know. Whose mother were you really? At the bottom of your heart, where your blood is red with pain, whom did you really love? No evil feelings, Ma, but, I mean a man has got to know. You see, he's been such a burden as a brother. [*Agitation.*] Don't be dumb. Don't cry! It was just a question! Look! I brought you a present, old soul. [*Holds out a hand with the fingers lightly closed.*] It's a butterfly. A real beauty butterfly. We were travelling fast, Ma. We hit them at ninety . . . a whole flock. But one was still alive, and it made me think of . . . Mother . . . So I caught it, myself, for you, remembering what I caught from you. This, old Ma of mine, is gratitude, and it proves it, doesn't it? Some things are only skin deep, because I got it, here in my hands, I got beauty . . . too . . . haven't I?

SCENE SEVEN

The next evening.

For the first time the room is untidy. The beds are not made, the table is cluttered, the floor littered with the strings and wrappings of the parcels of the previous day. Morris is alone. He sits lifelessly at the table, his head fallen on his chest, his arms hanging limp at his sides. On the table is a small bundle. Then Zachariah comes in. He behaves normally, going straight to the bed and taking off his shoes. Only when this is done does he realize something is wrong. The footbath hasn't been prepared.

ZACHARIAH. What's this? [*Looking around for the basin.*] Foot-salts finished? Hell, man! Couldn't you have seen? What must I do now? My feet are killing me, you know. [*Touching the toes.*] Forget the salts then. Just give me some hot. A soak will do them good.

[*Morris doesn't move.*]

Some hot, Morrie! Please!

[*Nothing happens.*]

Ag, no, man, don't tell me the stove is buggered up!

[*Goes to the stove and feels the kettle.*]

What the hell's happened? A man works all day, he comes home and finds this . . . [*The stove.*] . . . and this. [*The room.*] Floor not swept! Beds not made!

[*Beginning to realize. Morris struggles to find a word, but fails and drops his shoulders in a gesture of defeat and resignation. Disbelief.*]

You say nothing? [*A little laugh, but this quickly dies. Desperate.*] No, it's not funny. What happened?

MORRIS. I've given up.

ZACHARIAH. What?

MORRIS. I mean, I can't carry on.

ZACHARIAH. Oh, so you've just stopped, hey?

MORRIS. Yes.

ZACHARIAH. But that won't do! Emphatically not! A man can't stop just like that, like you. That's definitely no good, because, because . . . because a man must carry on. Most certainly. [*Sees the bundle on the table for the first time.*] What's this bundle, Morrie?

MORRIS. My belongings.

ZACHARIAH. What's that?

MORRIS. My Bible and my alarm clock. I was leaving, Zach.

ZACHARIAH. Leaving?

MORRIS. Going away.

ZACHARIAH. Where?

MORRIS. The road. Wherever it went.

ZACHARIAH. Oh! [*Pause.*] What about me?

MORRIS. I know, I know.

ZACHARIAH. But you don't care, hey?

MORRIS. I do care, Zach!

ZACHARIAH [*ignoring the denial*]. That's a fine thought for a loving brother. I'm surprised at you. In fact I'm shocked, shocked, shocked, shocked.

MORRIS. Stop it, Zach! I'm still here. I know I can't go . . . so I've given up instead. [*Pause.*]

ZACHARIAH. Come on, cheer up. It's not so bad.

MORRIS. I can't, Zach. Honestly I can't anymore.

ZACHARIAH. Hey, I've got a surprise for you.

MORRIS. It will have to be damn good to make any difference.

ZACHARIAH. How good is a letter from Ethel?

MORRIS. No damn good! You've missed the point, Zach. Don't you see, man! She's the blame.

[*Zachariah takes out the letter.*]
I don't want it. Take it away.

ZACHARIAH [*putting the letter down on the table so that Morris can see it*]. She's yours. I gave her to you.

MORRIS. Everything was fine until she came along.

ZACHARIAH. No, no, no. She hasn't yet.

MORRIS. What do you mean?

ZACHARIAH. Come along. You've missed the problem. Ethel coming along was the problem. She hasn't yet. But I mean, she might be on her way. I mean . . . it could be June, couldn't it? And one fine day, you know what? Another knock at the door. But it won't be me. So, you see, if I were you, just for safety's sake, of course, I'd have a quick peek at that letter.

[*Zachariah goes to his bed. Morris hesitates for a second, then takes the letter, opens it, and reads in silence. When he has finished he puts it down and looks at Zachariah vacantly. Zachariah is unable to contain himself any longer.*]

She's coming! What does she say? Wait! Let me guess. She's on the train, on her way, and it's June. When do you meet, man? What did she say? Tell me, Morrie?

MORRIS. No, Zach, prepare yourself for . . . good news. Ethel's gone and got engaged to get married, to Luckyman Stoffel.

ZACHARIAH. No.

MORRIS. S'true.

ZACHARIAH. No!

MORRIS. Then listen, Zach. [*Reads.*] 'Dear Pen-pal, it's sad news for you but good news for me. I've decided to get married. Ma says it's okay. The lucky man is Stoffel, who plays in my brother's team, fullback. It's a long story. Lucy thought she had him, but she didn't, so now we're not on talking terms no more. Stoffel works at Boetie's Garage and doesn't like competition so he says pen-pals is out if we're going to get married to each other. He's sitting here now and he says he wants to say this: "Leave my woman alone if you know what's good for you." That was Stoffel. He's a one all right. Well, pal, that's all for now, for ever. Ethel.' [*Pause.*] Down here at the bottom she says: 'You can keep the snapshot for a keepsake.'

[*Morris looks vacantly at Zachariah whose attitude has hardened with bitter disappointment.*]

ZACHARIAH. So?

MORRIS. So I think we can begin again, Zach.

ZACHARIAH. What?

MORRIS. That's a good question. [*Pause.*] Well, let's work it out. Where are we? Here. What is this? Our house. Me and you, Morrie and Zach . . . live here . . . in peace because the problem's gone . . . and got engaged to be married . . . and I'm Morrie . . . and I was going to go, but now I'm going to stay!

[*With something of his old self, Morris goes to work, opens his bundle and packs out his belongings.*]

Hey, Zach! [*Holding up the clock.*] It's stopped. Like me. What time shall we make it? Supper!

ZACHARIAH. I'm not hungry.

MORRIS. Bedtime?

ZACHARIAH. I don't want to sleep.

MORRIS. Just after supper, then. We'll say we've eaten.

ZACHARIAH. You can say what you like!

MORRIS. What's the matter, Zach?

ZACHARIAH [*slowly*]. You aren't going to wear that suit anymore?

MORRIS. I see. Zach, look at me now. Solemnly, on the holy Bible, I promise I won't.

ZACHARIAH. That's it.

MORRIS. What?

ZACHARIAH [*slyly*]. You looked so damn nice in that suit. It made me feel good.

MORRIS. You mean that?

ZACHARIAH. Cross my heart.

MORRIS. You mean you want to see me in it?

ZACHARIAH. *Ja.*

MORRIS. Be honest now, Zach. You are saying that you would like me to put that suit on?

ZACHARIAH [*emphatically*]. Now.

MORRIS. Now!

ZACHARIAH. *Ja!*

MORRIS. This comes as a surprise, Zach. But if as you say it makes you feel better . . . well . . . that just about makes it my duty, doesn't it? [*Moving to the suit.*] It was a damn good buy, Ethel or no Ethel. I really am tempted.

ZACHARIAH. Then get in.

MORRIS. Not so easy now . . . after yesterday. Say something to help me.

ZACHARIAH. Just for size. Just for the sake of the size, Morrie. Just for size. No harm done, Morrie. No harm done. We're only playing.

MORRIS. Only playing. That does it. Close your eyes, Zach!
[*With a laugh, Morris puts on the suit.*]

No peeking, Zach!
[*When he is dressed, he walks around the room in exaggerated style.*]
Zach!

ZACHARIAH [*encourages him*]. *Ek sê!* Just look! *Hoe's dit vir 'n ding! Links draai, regs swaai . . . Aitsa! Ou pellie,* you're stepping high tonight!

MORRIS [*stops, turns suddenly*]. Hey, *swartgat!*
[*A second of silence, and then Zachariah laughs.*]
No harm done now, hey, Zach?

ZACHARIAH. No pain.

MORRIS. That's the way to take a joke. Hey, *swartgat!*

ZACHARIAH [*playing along*]. *Ja, Baas?*

MORRIS. Who are you?

ZACHARIAH. Your boy, Zach, *Baas.*

MORRIS. And who am I?

ZACHARIAH. *Baas* Morrie, *Baas.*

MORRIS. *Baas* Morrie and his boy, Zach! My God, you're comical! Where'd you get that joke from, Zach?

ZACHARIAH. At the gate.

MORRIS. So that's what it's like.

ZACHARIAH. They're all dressed up smart like you, and go walking by. Come on, come. Try it. Walk past—

MORRIS. What?

ZACHARIAH. Walk past.

MORRIS. You want to play it?

ZACHARIAH. Why not?

MORRIS. I haven't seen the gate before, Zach. It's difficult to play something you haven't seen.

ZACHARIAH. I'll show you. Here it is. [*Vague gesture.*] This here is the gate.

MORRIS. What's on the other side?

ZACHARIAH. Does it matter?

MORRIS. It does if we're going to play this thing properly.

ZACHARIAH [*looking back*]. Trees.

MORRIS. Tall trees, with picnics in the shade.

ZACHARIAH. Grass.

MORRIS. Green. We'll make it spring.

ZACHARIAH. Flowers with butterflies.

MORRIS. That's a good touch, Zach.

ZACHARIAH. And benches.

MORRIS. How thoughtful! I'll want to rest.

ZACHARIAH. And I'm squatting here.

MORRIS. Right. So now you'll open the gate for me when I get there?

ZACHARIAH. No. It's open. I'll just watch your boots as you go by.

MORRIS. Then what's your job at the gate?

ZACHARIAH [*pause*]. They put me there to chase the black kids away.

[*Morris hesitates.*]

MORRIS. Are you sure we should play this?

ZACHARIAH. It's only a game. Walk past.

MORRIS. Just a game. No harm done.

[*He flourishes his umbrella and then saunters slowly towards Zachariah.*]

Shame! Look at that poor old boy. John? What are you doing . . . ?

ZACHARIAH [*cutting him*]. No, Morrie.

MORRIS. What's wrong?

ZACHARIAH. They never talk to me, man. Try it again.

[*Morris tries it again. This time he doesn't speak, but pretends to take a coin out of his pocket and tosses it to Zachariah.*]

How much?

MORRIS. Fifty cents.

ZACHARIAH. What!

MORRIS. Twenty cents.

ZACHARIAH. Too much.

MORRIS. Ten cents.

65

[*Zachariah is still doubtful.*]

All right then, a cent.

ZACHARIAH. *Ja*, that's a bit better, but—

MORRIS. But what?

ZACHARIAH. You think you're the soft sort of white man, giving me a cent like that.

MORRIS. What's wrong with being the soft sort? You find them.

ZACHARIAH. I know. But not with boots, Morrie. Never with boots. That sort doesn't even see me. Come on. Try it again.

[*The mime is repeated. This time Morris walks straight past.*]

MORRIS. Now what?

ZACHARIAH. I have a thought. I'm squatting here, and I think.

MORRIS. Okay.

ZACHARIAH. Bastard!

MORRIS [*sharply*]. Who?

ZACHARIAH. Don't spoil it, man! You can't hear me. It's just a thought.

[*Taps his forehead.*]

MORRIS [*looking away, frowning*]. Carry on.

ZACHARIAH. That's all.

MORRIS. Just . . .

ZACHARIAH. Just . . . Bastard!

MORRIS. What happens now?

ZACHARIAH. I'm watching you, remember? And you're looking up at the trees.

MORRIS. Yes, of course. It's a tall tree. I'm wondering if I've ever seen a tree as tall as this tree. There's also a great weight of birdies on its branches and . . . actually I'm finding difficulty keeping my mind up the tree with you behind my back. I feel your presence. So I think, I'll move further on . . . I mean, I'll have to get away if I want to admire the beauty, won't I? So I'll take this road. Yes. It's a good road. It's going places, because ahead of me I see the sky. I see it through the trees . . . so I'm climbing up a hill in this road, putting miles between us; and now, at last, ·there ahead of me is the sky, big, blue, beautiful; and I hurry on to the top where I turn against it and look back at you . . . far behind me now, in the distance, outside the gate. Can you see me?

ZACHARIAH. A little.

MORRIS. What is it you see here, in the distance, beyond the trees, upon the hill, against the sky?

ZACHARIAH. Can it be a . . . man?

MORRIS. A white man! Don't you see the way I stand? Didn't you see the way I walked? What do you think now?

ZACHARIAH. He's a bastard!

MORRIS [*reckless in his elation*]. Well, I don't care. It's too far away for me now to see your eyes. In fact, I'm almost free . . . So away I go, laughing, over the green spring grass, into the flowers and among the butterflies. And what do I say? What do I shout? Look at me, will you please! At last—I've changed! [*Pause.*] Now I'm tired. After so many years, so much beauty is a burden. I need rest. And here is one of those thoughtful benches. [*Sits.*] Ah, dearie, dearie me.

[*Zachariah comes past, bent low, miming the picking up of litter in the park. One hand trails a sack, the other is stabbing with a stick pieces of paper. Morris watches this with critical interest.*]

What are you doing?

ZACHARIAH. Picking up rubbish. I got a stick with a nail on the end. This is my rubbish bag. Every afternoon, at four o'clock, I go through the trees and around the benches and pick up the papers.

MORRIS. I thought I left you behind.

ZACHARIAH. I know.

MORRIS. The sight of you affects me, John.

ZACHARIAH [*continuing with his mime*]. I can feel it does.

MORRIS It's interesting. Just looking at you does it. I don't need the other senses. Just sight, just the sight of you crawling around like some . . . thing . . . makes me want to throw up.

ZACHARIAH. I know.

MORRIS [*rising*]. In fact I'd like to . . . [*Stops himself.*]

ZACHARIAH. Carry on.

MORRIS [*walking away*]. I can't.

ZACHARIAH. Why?

67

MORRIS. I'm telling you I can't.

ZACHARIAH. But, why?

MORRIS. Not with that old woman watching us.
    [*Zachariah stops and looks questioningly at Morris.*]
    Over there. [*Pointing.*]

ZACHARIAH. Old woman?

MORRIS. Horribly old.

ZACHARIAH. Alone?

MORRIS. All by her lonely self.

ZACHARIAH. And she's watching us?

MORRIS All the time. [*Impatience.*] Can't you see, Zach? She's wearing a grey dress on Sunday.

ZACHARIAH [*recognition dawning*]. Ah, soapsuds . . .

MORRIS. . . . on brown hands.

ZACHARIAH. And sore feet, hey! The toes are crooked.

MORRIS. She's been following me all day . . . begging!

ZACHARIAH. Call the police.

MORRIS. No, no. Not that.

ZACHARIAH. Then what will we do?

MORRIS. Let's work it out. We can't carry on with her watching us . . . behind that bush . . . like an old spy.

ZACHARIAH. So she must go.

MORRIS. I think so, too. [*A step in the direction of the old woman.*] Go away.

ZACHARIAH. Is she moving?

MORRIS. No. [*Trying again.*] Go away, old one! Begat and be gone! Go home! [*Sigh.*] It's no use. She won't listen to me.

ZACHARIAH [*trying to scare her off*]. Hey!

MORRIS [*excited*]. Ha, ha, she jumped!

ZACHARIAH. *Voetsek!*

MORRIS. Another jump.
    [*Zachariah goes down on his hands and knees.*]
    What are you doing?

ZACHARIAH. Stones.

MORRIS. Hoooooooo! She heard you. She's trotted off a little distance. But you're not really going to use them, are you?

ZACHARIAH. It's the only way. [*Throws.*]

MORRIS. Almost.

[*Zachariah throws again.*]

She jumped!

ZACHARIAH. *Voetsek!*

MORRIS. Yes. *Voetsek* off! We don't want you!

ZACHARIAH. Bugger off!

MORRIS. You old bitch! You made life unbearable!

ZACHARIAH [*starts throwing with renewed violence*]. *Hamba!*

MORRIS. She's running now.

ZACHARIAH. Get out!

MORRIS. *Kaffermeid!*

ZACHARIAH. *Ou hoer!*

MORRIS. *Luisgat!*

ZACHARIAH. *Swartgat!*

MORRIS. You've hit her! She's down. Look . . . look!

ZACHARIAH. Look at those old legs sticking up!

MORRIS. She's got no pants on! Get the hell out of here, you old bitch!

[*Their derision rises to a climax, Morris shaking his umbrella, Zachariah his fists.*]

That's the last of her I think. By God, she ran!

[*Pause while they get their breath.*]

Where were we?

ZACHARIAH. It was four o'clock. I was collecting the rubbish. You wanted to do . . . something.

MORRIS. That's right. I remember now. I just wanted to . . . just wanted to . . . poke you with my umbrella. He-he-he! [*He attacks Zachariah savagely.*] Just wanted to poke you a little bit. That's all. He-he! What do you think umbrellas are for when it doesn't rain? Hey?

[*Zachariah tries to escape, but Morris catches him with the crook of the umbrella.*]

Wait, wait! Not so fast, John. I want to have a good look at you. My God! What sort of mistake is this? A black man? All over, my boy?

ZACHARIAH. Sorry, *Baas.*

MORRIS. Your pits and privates?

ZACHARIAH. *Ja, Baas.*

MORRIS. Nothing white?

ZACHARIAH. Forgive me please, my *Baas.*

MORRIS. You're horrible.

ZACHARIAH. Sorry, *Baas.*

MORRIS. You stink.

ZACHARIAH. Please, my *Baasie* . . .

MORRIS. What did you mean crawling around like that? Spoiling the view, spoiling my chances! What's your game, hey? Trying to be an embarrassment? Is that it? A two-legged, bloody embarrassment? Well, we'll see about that. I hate you, do you hear? Hate! . . . Hate! . . . Hate! . . .

[*He attacks Zachariah savagely with the umbrella. When his fury is spent he turns away and sits down.*]

It was a good day. The sun shone. The sky was blue. I was happy. [*Smiling, released of all tensions.*] Not the sort of day to forget in a hurry. There's a spiny chill sprung up now, though. [*Shivering, Zachariah is moaning softly.*] Something sighing among the trees . . . must be the wind. Yes! There were trees as well today. The tall trees. So much to remember! Still . . . [*Shivering.*] . . . it is getting nippy . . . and I haven't got an overcoat . . . with me.

ZACHARIAH. Ding-dong . . . ong . . . ong . . . ding-dong . . . ong . . . ong.

MORRIS. What is that sound I hear?

ZACHARIAH. Bells. They're closing up now. Ding-dong . . . ong . . . ong.

MORRIS. Then I'd better hurry home. [*Stands.*] Yes, it was a good day . . . while it lasted.

ZACHARIAH. Ding-dong . . . ong . . . ong.

MORRIS. Ah, there's the gate.

ZACHARIAH. What's the matter with you?

MORRIS. What's the matter with me?

ZACHARIAH. Can't you see the gate is locked?

MORRIS. Is it? [*Tries the gate.*] It is.

ZACHARIAH. I locked it before I rang the bell.

MORRIS. Heavens above! Then I'd better climb over.

ZACHARIAH. Over those sharp pieces of glass they got on the top?

MORRIS. Then the fence.

ZACHARIAH. Barbed wire . . . very high . . .

MORRIS. So what do I do?

ZACHARIAH. You might try calling.

MORRIS. Hello! Hello, anybody there?

ZACHARIAH. Seems like nobody hears you, hey!

MORRIS. Now what?

ZACHARIAH. You think you'll try the gate on the other side.

MORRIS [*alarm*]. All the way back?

ZACHARIAH. Uh-huh. [*Moves quietly to the lamp on the table.*]

MORRIS. Through the trees?

ZACHARIAH. Looks like it. [*Turning down the lamp.*]

MORRIS. But it's getting dark.

ZACHARIAH. It happens every day.

MORRIS. And cold . . . and I never did like shadows . . . [*Pause.*] Where are you?

ZACHARIAH. Behind a tree.

MORRIS. But . . . but I thought you were the good sort of boy?

ZACHARIAH. Me?

MORRIS. Weren't you that? The simple, trustworthy type of John-boy. Weren't you that?

ZACHARIAH. I've changed.

MORRIS. Who gave you the right?

ZACHARIAH. I took it!

MORRIS. That's illegal! They weren't yours. That's theft. 'Thou shalt not steal.' I arrest you in the name of God. *Ja.* Please! [*Looking around wildly.*] My prayers . . .

[*Morris goes down on his knees. Zachariah begins to move to him.*]

71

Our Father, which art our Father in heaven, because we never knew the other one; forgive us this day our trespassing; I couldn't help it. The gate was open, God, so I didn't see the notice prohibiting! And 'beware of the dog' was in Bantu, so how was I to know, Oh, Lord! My sins are not that black. Furthermore, just some bread for the poor, daily, and please let your Kingdom come as quick as it can, for Yours is the power and the glory, ours is the fear and the judgment of eyes behind our back for the sins of our birth and the man behind the tree in the darkness while I wait . . . no, no, no—

[*Zachariah stands above Morris on the point of violence. The alarm clock rings. Morris crawls frantically away, then jumps up, rushes to the table and turns up the lamp. Zachariah goes to his bed and sits. A long silence. They avoid each other's eyes. Morris takes off the jacket. At the window:*]

Wind's coming up. It's the mystery of my life, that lake. I mean . . . It looks dead, doesn't it? If ever there was a piece of water that looks dead and done for, that's what I'm looking at now. Ah, well. Bedtime! [*Leaving the window.*] We'll sleep well tonight, you'll see.

ZACHARIAH. Morris?

MORRIS. Yes, Zach?

ZACHARIAH. What happened?

MORRIS. You mean?

ZACHARIAH. *Ja.*

MORRIS. We were carried away, as they would say, by the game . . . quite far, in fact. Mustn't get worried, though . . . it was only a game. I'm sure it's a good thing we got the game. Because we got a lot of time left, you know! [*Little laugh.*] . . . Stretching ahead . . . in here . . . [*Pause.*] . . . I'm not too worried. I mean, other men get by without a future. In fact, I think there's quite a lot of people getting by without futures these days.

[*Silence. Morris makes the last preparations for bed.*]

ZACHARIAH. Morris?

MORRIS. Yes, Zach?

ZACHARIAH. What is it, Morrie? You know, the two of us . . . in here?

72

MORRIS. Home.

ZACHARIAH. Is there no other way?

MORRIS. No, Zach. You see, we're tied together. It's what they call the blood knot . . . the bond between brothers.

[*Morris moves to his bed.*]

HELLO AND GOODBYE

Hello and Goodbye was first presented in the United States by Kermit Bloomgarden in association with Commonwealth United Entertainment and Jonathan Burrows at the Sheridan Square Playhouse, September 18, 1969, under the direction of Barney Simon. Production design was by William Ritman. The cast was as follows:

JOHNNIE .... *Martin Sheen*
HESTER .... *Colleen Dewhurst*

The play was originally presented at the Library Theatre, Johannesburg, South Africa, October 26, 1965, also directed by Barney Simon and with the following cast:

JOHNNIE .... *Athol Fugard*
HESTER .... *Molly Seftel*

CHARACTERS

JOHNNIE SMIT
HESTER SMIT, *his sister*

ACT ONE

A kitchen table and four chairs, lit by a solitary electric light hanging above.

On the table is a bottle of fruit squash, a jug of water, and a glass.

Slumped forward in one of the chairs is a man—his head resting face down on his arms on the table. He holds a spoon in one hand and is tapping it against the side of the glass.

About ten taps in silence, then. . . .

JOHNNIE [*counting as he taps*]. . . . fifty-five, fifty-six, fifty-seven, fifty-eight, fifty-nine, sixty!

[*Stops tapping.*]

Three hundred and. . . .

[*Pause.*]

Five minutes—become hours, become days . . . today! . . . Friday somethingth, nineteen . . . what? . . . sixty-three. One thousand nine hundred and sixty-three! Multiplied by twelve, by thirty, by twenty-four, by sixty . . .

[*Pause.*]

by sixty again! . . . gives you every second. Jee-sus! Millions.

[*Pause.*]

Yes, since Jeesus.

[*He starts tapping again but stops after only a few.*]

No! I'm wrong. It's six. Sixty goes six times into three hundred and sixty. It's six minutes!

[*Looks around.*]

Walls. The table. Chairs—three empty, one . . . occupied. Here and now. Mine. No change. Yes there is! Me. I'm a fraction older. More memories. All the others! Same heres mostly. Here. Other nows. Then, and then when this happened and that happened. My milestones, in here mostly. 'And then one day, after a long illness, his. . . .'

[*Pause. Softly.*]

Which art now in heaven.

[*Pause.*]

Nearly. On the tip of my tongue that time. Just don't rush it. The shock to the nervous system has got to wear off!

[*Stands and exits. Returns a few seconds later and goes back to the table but doesn't sit. When he speaks this time it is in a loud, unnaturally matter-of-fact voice.*]

When the sun shines again. . . .

[*Pause.*]

Tomorrow! God willing, if it's a nice day I'll go to the beach. Bottle of beer and a packet of lemon creams. Make it an outing. Break the monotony. Open the door and leave the house. Walk down Upper Valley Road, then along the river to the bridge. There I'll catch the Summerstrand bus. Number six, and upstairs for the view. Sit on the rocks and watch the waves. Drink the beer and eat the biscuits. Breathe in the breeze. Come back in the twilight, refreshed. A day will have passed.

[*Pause. Softly.*]

How many now?

[*Loud again.*]

As I was saying, back in the twilight. Along the river with the frogs croaking. Back home. No place like here. That's a lie. What's the odds? Walk in, put on the light, have a look-see, look the same . . . NO!

[*Pause.*]

A day will have passed. Emptier. It will be . . . emptier. Somehow it's getting empty. But how? And what? And cold! When was it I went and came back and it was emptier and cold and every thing . . . so still!
Here it comes again! Quick. Something else.

[*He grabs the spoon on the table and starts tapping.*]

One two three four. . . .

[*Grabs the bottle.*]

Lemon squash! Ten tablespoons if there's a drop. Shake the bottle well before use! All the goodness sinks to the bottom! For quick relief of all, or eases, some say soothes. Depends on the pain. Change The Subject!

[*Notices there is some squash left in the glass.*]

Quench my thirst!

[*He drinks. Pause.*]

78

Am I going mad? No. This is not madness. Those who are, don't know they're mad. Whereas I know . . . I'm mad.

[*Pause.*]

Something wrong there. If you think you're mad you're not. That's it! Only when you think you aren't.

[*Exits and returns, but not to the table. He stops just inside the light.*]

It was the weight that shocked me. Suddenly so heavy! Why didn't I notice? All those times. My arms never ached. But they grunted. Sarel. The one called the other Sarel. 'Let's try it this way, Sarel,' he said. 'You go first.' One two three UP! In black suits with him weighing a weight that made them grunt and me . . . hanging around . . . my two helping hands useless and empty; all of me useless and big and getting in the way when they tried to get him through the door . . . excuse me try it again sorry am I in the way OOOOps gently does it don't drop it I beg your pardon your forgiveness your sorrow. . . . Suddenly they were out, going, and everybody on the pavement was staring at me. . . . Isn't there something to sign, I asked. A form to fill? We've got your name and address, he said. The office will contact you. So that was that. One two three UP! Picked up and carried out. Pushed in the back. Carried away. Bumping up and down because the road is bad. Finally just a thing. Horribly heavy. IT. Smothered by a sheet. Shoved in a hole. . . .

[*Desperate move to the table—grabs the spoon and starts tapping.*]

If this isn't madness it's a nervous breakdown. Think! Anything!

[*Tries to pour himself some squash.*]

Quick quench!

[*He can't get the stopper off the bottle fast enough.*]

Too late. HELP!

[*He grabs hold of the edge of the table, closes his eyes, and starts to speak at a very fast tempo—the first part of the speech is almost gabbled.*]

Queen Victoria's statue is on the square and during the day pigeons sit on it and do their business on it so looking up she said thank god cows don't fly but we've heard that one before and between shifts the bus conductors sit under it on benches with little tin boxes waiting for their buses with boxes on benches buses bunches of bosses all routes here we Go. . . .

[*Takes a deep breath.*]

Summerstrand Humewood Cadles Walmer Perridgevale Newton Park Mount Pleasant Kensington Europeans only and all classes double deckers with standing prohibited spitting prosecuted and alighting while in motion is at your own risk. . . .

[*Tempo gradually slowing down.*]

And sooner or later it starts to get dark in the square, the sun sets, the last light goes riding away on the backs of the buses, and then it's twilight with a sky stretching all the way down Main Street and beyond who knows where, the ends of the earth. . . . And all being well I'm in the gloom on Jetty Street corner watching while it gathers, waiting for nothing in particular with the City Hall clock telling the time, some time, ding-dong, start to count forget to finish because it's all the same . . . the cars get fewer, the newspaper boys stop calling and count their pennies on the pavement while darkness is coming it seems from the sea up Jetty Street. . . . Bringing peace, the end of the day, my moment, everybody hurrying away from it, leaving it, for me, just me, there in the shadows and no questions asked, for once enough, ME is enough, need nothing, whisper my name without shame. . . . Until the lights go on. . . . Suddenly like a small fright, ON, which is my sign to think of going. . . . Which I do. . . . I pull up my roots as the saying goes and go. . . . Down Baakens Street past the police station where the bars on the windows and the pick-up vans give me the creeps. . . . To Baakens Bridge. . . . And near the bus-sheds there, one night . . . I saw a bus-conductor off duty pressing a girl against the wall in a dark corner and he was smiling and holding his time-sheet and she looked sly and then he kissed her. . . . Black water was under the bridge running the wrong way because of the sea. . . . While he kissed her and smiled and she was sly. . . . While he held his time-sheet. . . .

[*Speaking now at an even tempo—each image distinct.*]

And not far away from there I will hear the frogs, without fail, the frogs never fail. In the meantime I hear trains shunting and try not to remember something; with the sky getting darker all this time and an old woman sitting with oranges under a lamp-post not selling any. . . . And me, me, walking, pressing on, I'm. . . .

[*Long pause. He opens his eyes.*]

Safe. Yes. Sure enough. Safe and sound. Firm ground. That was close. Like a hole, black and deep, among all the little thoughts. Suddenly there's nothing, and I'm falling! These are dangerous days. Safety first. Arrive in peace not in pieces. Bloody good!

[*Exits and returns.*]

So he kissed her. Just like that. And I thought, there are things to think about, which I did and still do, things to happen which hadn't and don't seem to. Other things happen to me. I am not complaining. I'm happy with my lot.

[*Pause.*]

My little.

So where were we?

[*Vigorous and clear, as if directing a stranger.*]

After the bridge turn sharp right. Carry on along the foot of the cliff until you come to a fork. Take the bottom prong. Then third to your left. It's on the left-hand side about half-way up. Fifty-seven A. You can't miss it. Green windows and a door . . .

. . . a door I never knock. Because it's my door. Open it with . . . some sort of heart and my right hand, close it with my left hand, behind me. Stand and listen. What sort of heart? Beating loud. Listening.

Stop! Just stop. Easy does it. Count the chairs. One two three four chairs. Table. One man. Friday somethingth. Move. Keep moving. Look for light entertainment.

[*Exits left and returns almost immediately with a comic.*]

Seen like that life's amazing!

[*He sits and reads the comic.*]

[*A woman appears up stage and walks slowly into the light. She is wearing a coat and carrying a large and battered suitcase. This is* Hester. *Johnnie looks up from his comic and watches her.*]

HESTER [*putting down the suitcase*]. Hello.

JOHNNIE. Hello.

HESTER. Didn't you hear me calling?

JOHNNIE. No.

HESTER. Well I did!

JOHNNIE. I'm not arguing.

HESTER. I thought nobody was home.

JOHNNIE. No. I've been sitting here, minding my own business. . . .

HESTER. Well then listen next time, for God's sake. First the taxi hooted. But he was in a hurry so I told him to drop me. I could see the light was on.

JOHNNIE. I've been reading. . . .

HESTER. I even started to wonder if it was the right place.

JOHNNIE. Fifty-seven A Valley Road. Smit's the name.

HESTER. You being funny? Anyway the door wasn't locked. So what you got to say for yourself?

JOHNNIE. Surprised of course. I mean, put yourself in my shoes. I'm sitting here, reading a comic, passing the time, and then you! Suddenly you're here too.

HESTER. Not even a word of welcome.

[*Pause.*]

JOHNNIE. Welcome.

HESTER. Don't kill yourself!

JOHNNIE. Make yourself at home!

HESTER. I will.

JOHNNIE. What else? HospitaliTEA! How about a nice cup of. . . . No. Milk's finished. Can I offer you a refreshing glass of lemon squash? It's preserved with Benzoic Acid.

HESTER. Later.

[*She moves right and stares off in that direction.*]

Sleeping?

JOHNNIE. Who?

HESTER. Who? Him! Is he sleeping? Hell, you just woken up or something?

JOHNNIE. Me? No. I've been sitting here, reading. . . .

HESTER. Okay, okay. How's things otherwise?

JOHNNIE. Just a comic, mind you. Not a book. I've run out of reading-matter.

HESTER. I didn't come a thousand miles to talk about comics.

JOHNNIE. So?

HESTER. So change the subject.

JOHNNIE. There's no law against reading a comic in my own home.

HESTER. All right.

JOHNNIE. I admitted it wasn't a book.

HESTER. All right I said.

JOHNNIE. But I'm not harming anyone.

HESTER. For God's sake, all right. Read your bloody comic. All I wanted was a word of welcome. Is that asking so much? Look, let's start again. Have a cigarette.

[*They light cigarettes.*]

I'm leaving it to you.

JOHNNIE. What?

HESTER. The questions.

JOHNNIE. What questions?

HESTER. Or news.

JOHNNIE. No news, good news.

HESTER. Who cares? Let's hear it.

JOHNNIE. What?

HESTER. Anything. Just talk!

JOHNNIE. Okay.

HESTER. Good.

JOHNNIE. Can I be frank?

HESTER. Go ahead.

JOHNNIE. What do you want?

HESTER. How the hell do you like that!

JOHNNIE. I'm not telling you to go. Stay as long as you like.

I admire your—what's the word?—pluck. I always admire people who pluck up courage and barge in. But still—you and your suitcase, out of the blue, the dark, on my doorstep and before I could blink an eye in my house! You follow? What's all this in aid of?

HESTER. Listen to him!

JOHNNIE. Look, I said you could stay. I'm just interested. . . .

HESTER. Are you mad?

JOHNNIE. See what I mean. Straight to the point. Anyway, me mad? I worked it out. I don't think I am, therefore. . . . No . . . those that think they are . . . to cut a long story short I'm not.

HESTER. Johnnie?

JOHNNIE. You even know my name.

HESTER. Am I hearing you right? Of course I know your name.

[*Pause.*]

I don't believe it.

JOHNNIE. Truth is stranger than fiction.

HESTER. You don't know who I am.

JOHNNIE. You got me guessing.

HESTER. Don't you recognize me at all?

JOHNNIE. I admit I haven't had a really good look yet. I start with the feet and work up.

HESTER. Shut up! So why did you just sit there? Why didn't you ask?

JOHNNIE. But I did. I asked you. . . .

HESTER. All right!

[*Pause.*]

I'm Hester. Your sister, Hester Smit.

[*Pause.*]

Didn't you get my letter?

JOHNNIE. What letter?

HESTER. I wrote. Fifty-seven A Valley Road, Port Elizabeth. Saying I was coming. I waited and waited for a reply. Didn't you get it?

84

JOHNNIE. No.

HESTER. Well, I'm Hester, and I come back to visit you, Johnnie, my brother. So what you waiting for? Don't you believe me?

JOHNNIE. Give me time.

HESTER. I'm Hester, I tell you!

JOHNNIE. Prove it.

HESTER. You got a sister called Hester, haven't you?

JOHNNIE. Yes.

HESTER. And she's been gone a long time?

JOHNNIE. Yes.

HESTER. Well, that's me.

JOHNNIE. So prove it.

HESTER. You got a birthmark there . . .

[*Pointing.*]

. . . what looks like the map of Africa upside down; and on your leg, your left leg I think—yes it is!—there's an operation from that time you were playing with the Boer War bullet and it went off. Are you satisfied?

JOHNNIE. But all of that's me. I know I'm Johnnie. It's *you.* You say you're Hester. Prove it.

HESTER. I'll hit you.

JOHNNIE. No you won't.

HESTER. How the hell would I know all about you if I wasn't me? If I wasn't Hester? I came *here*, didn't I? I know the address, your name, about him. . . .

[*Pointing off-right. Pointing off-left.*]

That was our room; this was a lounge-cum-kitchen but after Mommie died I went on growing which isn't good for little boys to see so you moved in here and then it was kitchen-cum-bedroom, which also didn't matter because mostly there was a row on the go and nobody was talking to anybody else. Right or wrong? And when you got big and Daddy got worse it was you used to look after him because I was working at the Astoria Café, and that's his room and he's lying there with only one leg left because of the explosion; and all our life it was groaning and moaning and what the

85

Bible says and what God's going to do and I hated it!
Right or wrong? Right! And it was hell. I wanted to scream.
I got so sick of it I went away. What more do you want?
Must I vomit?

[*Pause.*]

Well, don't just stand there. Take a good look and see it's me.

[*Hester moves close to Johnnie—she sees him properly for the first
time. When she speaks again it is with the pain of recognition—
what is and what was.*]

Johnnie! It's been a long time, *boetie.*

[*A small impulsive gesture of tenderness—hand to his cheek?—
which she breaks off abruptly. She moves away.*]
[*Flat, matter-of-fact voice.*]

Well, is it me?

JOHNNIE [*quiet certainty*]. Yes, it's you.

HESTER. You sure?

JOHNNIE. I'm certain.

HESTER. Hester Smit.

JOHNNIE. I remember. . . .

HESTER. My face hasn't changed?

JOHNNIE. . . . your hate! It hasn't changed. The sound of it.
Always so sudden, so loud, so late at night. Nobody else
could hate it the way you did.

HESTER [*weary scorn*]. This? Four walls that rattled and a roof
that leaked! What's there to hate?

JOHNNIE. Us.

HESTER. I've got better things to do with my hate.

JOHNNIE. You hated something. You said so yourself.

HESTER. All right, something. The way it was! All those years,
and all of us, in here.

JOHNNIE. Then why have you come back?

HESTER. That was twelve years ago.

JOHNNIE. You don't hate it now?

HESTER. Now. What's now? I've just arrived.

JOHNNIE. Tonight.

HESTER. I'll tell you tomorrow. Let me look at it in the light.

JOHNNIE. How long will you be staying?

HESTER [*ignoring the question*]. *Ja.* Twelve years ago next month. I worked it out in the train. I was twenty-two. Best thing I ever did getting out of here.

JOHNNIE. Then why have you come back?

HESTER. You got lots of questions all of a sudden!

JOHNNIE. You said. . . .

HESTER. To hell with what I said. I'm here.

[*Looking around.*]

Mind you it's easier than I thought.

JOHNNIE. I've noticed that. It's always easier than we think.

HESTER. I thought it would be hard, or hurt—something like that. But here I am and it isn't so bad.

JOHNNIE. It's never as bad as we think.

HESTER. Do you know what I'm talking about?

JOHNNIE. No.

HESTER. Then shut up and listen!

[*Pause.*]

I'm talking about coming back. You see I tried hell of a hard to remember. That was a mistake. I got frightened.

JOHNNIE. Of what?

HESTER. Not like that. Maybe frightened is wrong. Don't get any ideas I'm scared of you lot. Just because I come back doesn't mean I'm hard-up. But at Kommodagga there was a long stop—I started remembering and that made me. . . .

[*Groping for words.*]

. . . I think 'nerves' is better. The whole business was getting on my nerves! The heat, sitting there sweating and waiting! I'm not one for waiting. It was the slow train, you see. All stops. And then also this old bitch in the compartment. I hate them when they're like that—fat and dressed in black like Bibles because somebody's dead, and calling me *Ou* Sister. I had her from Noupoort and it was non-stop all the time about the Kingdom of Heaven was at hand and swimming on Sunday and all that rubbish.

Because I was remembering, you see! It wasn't that I couldn't. I could. It was seeing it again that worried me. The same.

Do you understand? Coming back and seeing it all still the same. I wasn't frightened of there being changes. I said to myself, I hope there is changes. Please let it be different, and strange, even if I get lost and got to ask my way. I won't mind. But to think of it all still the same, the way it was, and me coming back to find it like that . . . ! Sick! It made me sick on the stomach. There was fruit cake with the afternoon tea and I almost vomited.

And every time just when I'm ready to be brave *Ou* Sister starts again on the Kingdom and Jesus doesn't like lipstick. By then I had her in a big way. So when she asks me if I seen the light I said no because I preferred the dark! Just like that, and I went outside to stand in the gangway. But next stop I see it's still only Boesmanspoort and ninety miles to go so it all starts again. Only it's worse now, because I start remembering like never before.

Those windy days with nothing to do; the dust in the street! Even the colour of things—so clear, man, it could have been yesterday. The way the grass went grey around the laundry drain on the other side, the foam in the river, and inside those Indian women ironing white shirts. And the smell, that special ironing smell—warm and damp—with them talking funny Indian and looking sad. Smells! I could give you smells a mile long—backyard smells, Sunday smells, and what about the Chinaman shop on the corner! Is he still there? That did it. Don't ask me why—something to do with no pennies for sweets—but that did it. If it's still there I said, if there's still those sacks of beans and sugar and rice on the floor with everything smelling that special way when I walk past, I'll bring up on the spot like a dog, so help me God.

So then I said, No, this isn't wise. Get off at Coega and catch the next one back to Jo'burg. Send them a telegram, even if it's a lie—sick of something, which was almost true. I was ready to do it. 'Strue's God!

But the next stop was Sandflats and there suddenly I see it's sunset. Somebody in the gangway said we were two hours late and it will be dark when we get in. That will help me, won't it, I think to myself. And it did. Because it was—dark and me feeling like a stranger in the taxi.

All my life I been noticing this, the way night works, the

way it makes you feel home is somewhere else. Even with
the lights on, like now, looking at this . . . I don't know. It is
and it isn't. I'm not certain. It could be true. Tomorrow
will tell. I never have doubts in daylight.
So that was that. Jo'burg to P.E. second class. Over to you.

JOHNNIE. Why have you come back?

[*Hester lights a cigarette, giving no sign of replying to the question.*]
That was a very good description. My journey to P.E. on the
S.A.R. I'd give you eight out of ten.

[*Pause.*]
Why have you come back?

HESTER. It's also my home. I've got a right to come here if
I want to. I'm still his daughter. How is he?

JOHNNIE. How long you staying?

HESTER. What you worried about? I'll buy my own food.

JOHNNIE. Is this a holiday? Back home for old times sake
sort of thing. Two weeks annually.

HESTER. In here? I got better things to do with my holidays.

JOHNNIE. So why have you come?

HESTER. Look, stop worrying! I'm passing through. It's hello
and goodbye. Maybe I'm gone tomorrow.

[*Looking off-right to father's room.*]
And him?

[*Johnnie stares at her.*]
Speak up! I don't care what you say.

[*Pause.*]
So he still hates me. I wasn't expecting miracles. Any case I
also got a memory. Don't think I've forgotten some of the
things that was said in here. It's my life and I'll do what
I like.

JOHNNIE. Yes, he still hates you. He doesn't want to see you.

HESTER. So what? Just remember Mommie didn't hate me
and half of this house was hers so I'm entitled to be here.
You can tell him that from me.

JOHNNIE. He's sleeping.

HESTER. I heard he was in a bad way.

JOHNNIE. He's sleeping in there.

HESTER. I know he's sleeping in there! But I heard he was in a bad way.

[*Pause.*]

Well, is it true?

JOHNNIE. No.

HESTER. I met old Magda Swanepoel and she told me nobody ever sees him any more and that she heard he was in a bad way. Death's door. Those were her words.

JOHNNIE. NO!

HESTER. So then tell me what's happening.

JOHNNIE. He's recovering.

HESTER. Well, it can't last for ever.

JOHNNIE. He's making a splendid recovery! Improving day by day. I've got him on Wilson's Beef and Iron tonic—one tablespoon with water after every meal. It's working wonders. Building up his strength. . . .

HESTER. But he's still cripple.

JOHNNIE. Yes.

HESTER. Still in bed most of the time.

JOHNNIE. Yes.

HESTER. Don't tell him I'm here. I'll be quiet. I'm not scared of him! But I can't stay long. Maybe tomorrow. Like I said it's just hello and goodbye. Anyway, let's see. Yes.

[*To her suitcase, which she opens, taking out a small packet.*]

There's no hard feelings between us so I bought you a present. We got on well together, didn't we?

[*Hands it over to Johnnie.*]

Well, aren't you going to open it? What's the matter with you, man? You never used to be like this. It's a cigar called a cheroot. Put one in your mouth and let's see. Oh well. . . . What else?

[*Back to her suitcase, rummaging through its contents.*]

I had some tea left, and this tin of condensed milk. Jam. It all helps. You want a pot? Here. I'm damned if I was going to leave her anything.

JOHNNIE. Who?

HESTER. Mrs. Humphries. Trocadero Court. The landlady. As it is she gets . . . let's see. I'm paid up till the end of the month. Ten days! By rights she owes me.

[*Back to the suitcase.*]

My own knife and fork. Spoon. Plate. That's all.

[*Rummaging.*]

Just my clothes.

JOHNNIE [*watching her*]. You've come back for something, Hester.

HESTER. Have I?

JOHNNIE. What?

HESTER. I didn't say yes.

JOHNNIE. I say you've come back for something.

HESTER. You can say what you like, my boy.

JOHNNIE. I know you.

HESTER. You know me, do you? Ten minutes ago you were singing another song.

[*Standing.*]

I feel dirty. Still the old zinc bath from the yard and a kettle of hot?

JOHNNIE. Yes.

HESTER. *Ag*, it can wait. I'm too tired. I suppose you're in my room now?

JOHNNIE. You take it.

HESTER. I'll be all right in here.

JOHNNIE. No! You take the bed. He needs me. He calls.

[*Pause.*]

HESTER. Yes. I remember that too. Late . . . *late* at night, when everybody was in bed, groaning or calling softly, on and on. . . .

JOHNNIE. He never called for you!

HESTER. I heard him all the same. Don't you hate it?

JOHNNIE. I don't know . . . NO! I don't hate it. I don't think about it. He's my father.

91

[*Hester breaks off staring at Johnnie and struggles off-left with her suitcase. Johnnie remains motionless at the table. Hester reappears a few seconds later.*]

HESTER. You're going to empty those slops in there sometime, I hope?

[*Exit Johnnie left with Hester following.*]

Christ Almighty, no wonder!

[*Johnnie reappears carrying a white enamel bucket.*]

[*Off.*]

And leave it out. Let it get some fresh air!

[*Exit Johnnie up stage. Returns to the table, empty-handed.*]

[*Off.*]

I can't understand why you never got that letter! I posted it. Fifty-seven A Valley Road. Where the hell is my. . . ?

[*Indistinct mumble of words—occasional phrases are heard.*]

. . . good ironing . . . second class . . . all that dust . . . one thing about a good drip-dry. . . .

[*Again loud and distinct.*]

Hell, man, why don't you get the broom in here? It's inches thick. I'm not fussy but this is the bloody limit. Just look at it!

JOHNNIE. Sssssh!

[*Hester appears in her petticoat.*]

He's sleeping.

HESTER. I wasn't making so much noise.

JOHNNIE. He needs all the sleep he can get.

HESTER. So who's stopping him?

JOHNNIE. You were shouting. The doctor said. . . .

HESTER. I know, I know. Good night.

[*Exit Hester. Johnnie waits a few seconds, listening, then follows her to the edge of light.*]

Close your door. Just in case.

[*As soon as he is satisfied that Hester has closed her door, Johnnie moves quickly to the table and looks wildly around the room. Hurried exit into father's room, returning immediately but stopping just inside the light to stare at Hester's room. Another impulsive move, this time*]

*to the table to collect two chairs which he stacks up at the entrance
to the father's room, blocking it. But he almost immediately changes
his mind and takes them back to the table.*]

JOHNNIE. Hester, back in the land of the living. It's her all
right. Large as life. Loud as . . . something. Bold! And not
answering questions. The danger signal! Hold your breath
and wait. What else? Think. Go back . . . back . . . all the
days, right back, further than I've ever been . . . memories.
Wind, as she said. Dust, and nothing to do . . . and Hester!
I'm crying and she's got her fingers in her ears. Does that
help me? Her fingers in her ears, and shouting or singing at
the top of her voice to drown my crying. How does that
help me? Or those times . . . saying nothing! That way of hers
—can't sit still, ants in her pants and saying nothing. Hester
with a scheme up her sleeve. There's a word—beer does it
in the dark—Brewing! And then trouble. Without fail. She
wants something. The letter!

[*Johnnie exits up stage, returning a few seconds later with a bundle
of mail—mostly commercial circulars. He goes through them hurriedly
and finds a letter, but before he can open it Hester reappears, smoking
a cigarette, a small mirror in her hand. Johnnie quickly tucks the
letter back into the pile of mail on the table.*]

HESTER. What you up to?

JOHNNIE [*picking up one of the commercial circulars*]. Boswell's
Circus. Behind the new Law Courts. Cheap seats five bob.

HESTER. Do you sit up all night?

JOHNNIE. When he's bad.

HESTER. You said he was better.

JOHNNIE. He's getting better.

HESTER. So he was bad.

JOHNNIE. Well on the road to recovery.

HESTER. But he *was*. . . .

JOHNNIE. We mustn't talk loud.

HESTER. I'm not talking loud.

JOHNNIE. I'm just saying.

HESTER. Well say it when I'm talking loud!

JOHNNIE. You're starting.

HESTER. Oh shit!

JOHNNIE. Why don't you get a good night's rest?

HESTER. Are you trying to get rid of me?

JOHNNIE. You look tired.

HESTER. Just now. It's those damn frogs. Were they always so loud?

JOHNNIE. Croak.

HESTER. What?

JOHNNIE. Ducks quack, dogs bark, frogs croak.

HESTER. All right, professor. I still don't remember them being so loud.

JOHNNIE. Some nights they don't croak at all.

[*Back to the mail.*]

Spick! 'Spick for your pots
    Spick for your pans
    Cleans like a shot
    And soft on the hands.'

They're damned clever, you know.

HESTER. There is something I want to ask you.

JOHNNIE. Now in a family pack.

HESTER. Hey! I've got a question.

JOHNNIE. As long as it's not loud.

HESTER. For God's sake! I'm talking at the bottom of my voice.

[*Johnnie goes back to the circular.*]

I haven't asked my question yet! What do *I* look like? When you saw me, and you knew it was me, Hester, did you remember much?

JOHNNIE. Like what?

HESTER. Like I was. I mean, am I changed much?

JOHNNIE [*not looking at her*]. Hard to say. . . .

HESTER. Have you had a good look at me yet?

JOHNNIE. It's the light in here. I feel it when I'm reading. Maybe I need glasses.

HESTER. Rubbish! Look at me. Come close! You're not looking properly! I can see it in your eyes.

94

JOHNNIE. I'm trying to.

HESTER. What's the matter with you?

JOHNNIE. It's rude to stare.

HESTER. I'm asking you to. Now come on!

JOHNNIE. All right, but don't stare at me. Look the other way.
  [*Pause. He looks at Hester.*]
  Okay.

HESTER. Well?

JOHNNIE. What do you want me to say?

HESTER. What you saw.

JOHNNIE. You—my sister Hester—a few years older. Satisfied?

HESTER. No! Am I also . . . were you shocked? At the changes?
  My face?
  [*Mirror in her hand.*]
  What do I really look like now? I can't see myself. Mirrors
  don't work. I can't watch . . . Me. When I look, *I* look back.

JOHNNIE [*back to the commercial circular*]. One cap-full is enough
  for a sink-full of dishes. That's a hell of a lot of dishes. One
  sink-full! Big families I suppose, and three meals a day.
  Porridge, stews, puddings. You'd need it then. Anything with
  gravy or fat, or soft fried eggs with that yellowy yolk. Once
  it's cold you've had it. As for the pot you've boiled milk
  in . . . ! Bread's the best. Dust off the plate and use it again.
  Also cheese, very hard-boiled eggs, biscuits—anything that
  comes in crumbs. Watch out for jam. It looks easy but once
  it's on the plate. . . .

HESTER. And you, Johnnie?

JOHNNIE. If I could afford it beer and lemon creams three
  times a day.

HESTER. Johnnie!

JOHNNIE. I'm all ears.

HESTER. What happened to you?

JOHNNIE. Who said anything happened to me?

HESTER. All these years! Wasn't it learner-stoker once upon
  a time? At the Kroonstad Railway School? You had the
  forms to fill in and everything. Then I left. What happened?

[*Johnnie is staring straight ahead.*]

Ever since I can remember you always wanted to be an engine driver. What. . . .

JOHNNIE. Sssssssh!

[*Exit into father's room. Returns a few seconds later but doesn't sit.*]

He's sleeping soundly. I gave him a dose of Wilson's Beef and Iron after supper. Instructions on the label. One tablespoon with water after meals. Here's the bottle if you don't believe me. Satisfied?

[*He sits.*]

HESTER. I'm not interested in him. I was asking what happened to you.

JOHNNIE. And I heard you. That was a long time ago. But I remember now. I changed my mind.

HESTER [*not believing him*]. Just like that!

JOHNNIE. Just like that.

HESTER. After all those years?

JOHNNIE. After all those years one morning I changed my mind just like that and didn't go. I tore up the application forms.

[*Back to the mail on the table.*]

We've had Spick, Boswell's Circus . . . what's left? Providential Assurance. Looks like arithmetic. And this?

[*The letter is uncovered.*]

Is this your handwriting?

HESTER. Give here. Hey, yes. This is it.

JOHNNIE [*taking it back*]. Let's see what you said.

[*He opens it.*]

HESTER. But I posted that weeks ago.

JOHNNIE. Isn't there something called surface mail?

HESTER [*watching him open the envelope*]. You going to read it?

JOHNNIE. You wrote it to me.

HESTER. No, wait. That's not fair.

JOHNNIE. Fair?

HESTER. I'm already here.

JOHNNIE. That makes it even fairer. You know . . . in your presence.

HESTER. I said wait! Let me think. NO. Hand over.

JOHNNIE. Strictly speaking it's mine now.

HESTER. Give it!

[*She grabs it out of his hands.*]

I want to read it first.

[*Hester reads the letter. Johnnie waits passively for a few seconds, then starts his next speech while she is reading.*]

JOHNNIE. Yes, it all comes back. Clear as daylight—which it was. Just after breakfast, in fact. I changed my mind! There are bigger things in life than driving an engine, I said. So I tore up the forms in duplicate, and never looked back. It's best, they say, and they're right. I never do. Habit. One of those that help. Good and bad. Onward, always onward. Eyes on the road. Leave the corner and over the bridge, under the cliffs and along the river and no regrets. I never look back. I'll see it all again tomorrow. Always onwards. That's me in a nutshell.

HESTER [*folding up the letter*]. Nothing much. I wouldn't worry about it if I was you.

JOHNNIE [*holding out his hand*]. Who cares?

HESTER [*ignoring the hand*]. Stick to your comics if you want a laugh. It's not worth reading.

JOHNNIE. Let's see what you said.

HESTER. Just that I'm coming by train.

JOHNNIE. Two pages.

HESTER. And how are you and I'm okay. The usual.

JOHNNIE. Two pages on both sides.

HESTER. Mrs. Humphries only had two pages left.

JOHNNIE. So it's really four pages to say you're coming by train and how am I and you're okay.

HESTER. And news.

JOHNNIE. What news?

HESTER. Just news, for God's sake. Don't you know what news is? Anyway you wouldn't be interested.

JOHNNIE. Then why did you write it?

HESTER. You got to write something.

JOHNNIE. I am interested. I've thought about it. I am definitely interested.

HESTER. All right. Don't panic. Remember Pearl Harbour. I said. . . .

JOHNNIE [*holding out his hand*]. Let me read it.

HESTER. I want to have another look.

JOHNNIE. I'll give it back.

HESTER. What you in such a hurry for?

JOHNNIE. I'm not in a hurry.

HESTER. Oh no? Look at your hand.

JOHNNIE [*withdrawing his hand*]. I'll wait.

[*He waits. Hester watches him.*]

HESTER. If you're trying to be funny, Johnnie Smit . . . !

[*Johnnie waits.*]

I'm warning you!

[*Johnnie waits.*]

Right, you asked for it!

[*Tearing up the letter.*]

That . . . and that . . . and that . . . and may God strike me stone dead if I ever write you another one.

[*She lights a cigarette; the letter has brought a tension to her.*]

JOHNNIE. Happy?

HESTER. Why should I be happy?

JOHNNIE. You didn't want me to read it.

HESTER [*vindictive*]. Yes! I didn't want you to read it.

JOHNNIE. That's what I said.

HESTER. And now you *can't* read it.

JOHNNIE. And that's why you're happy.

HESTER. Happy? In here? Don't make me laugh. Nothing in here knows what happy means.

JOHNNIE. 'That way of hers . . . saying nothing!'

HESTER. Who?

JOHNNIE. Hester with a scheme up her sleeve! What was in that letter?

HESTER. My own business.

JOHNNIE. Why didn't you want me to read it?

HESTER. Because it's going to stay my own business.

JOHNNIE. Suppose I found it before you arrived?

HESTER. Suppose, suppose. Suppose I didn't come, what then? Suppose he was dead, what then?

JOHNNIE. You Must Not Say That!

HESTER. I said suppose, for God's sake.

JOHNNIE. He's our father.

HESTER. Here we go again! And I'm his daughter and you're his son and I'm your sister and where's our mother? Well, I'm also ME! Just ME. Hester. And something is going to be mine—just mine—and no sharing with brothers or fathers. . . .

JOHNNIE. Twenty years ago you used to say that.

[*This remark stops her tirade. She moves about restlessly.*]
What are you looking for?

HESTER. I'm not looking for anything.

JOHNNIE. You're looking in all the corners.

HESTER. Twenty years ago. That puts him in his sixties.

JOHNNIE. All the corners—not answering questions.

HESTER. I said that puts him in his sixties.

JOHNNIE. Does it?

HESTER. Work it out.

JOHNNIE. Multiplied by. . . .

HESTER. Add.

JOHNNIE. Multiplication gives you the seconds.

HESTER. Just add. Middle age plus twenty years. Puts him in his old age. He must be getting grey then. Eyesight bad and the shakes. Isn't he grey?

JOHNNIE [*his eyes closed*]. . . . become minutes, become hours, days of the week. . . .

HESTER. Answer me! Is he grey?

JOHNNIE. Ssssssh!

[*Gets up and goes into father's room. Hester waits, lights another cigarette. After a few seconds Johnnie returns.*]

JOHNNIE. I thought I heard a groan. But he's still asleep. That doesn't mean he didn't groan. Sometimes he groans in his sleep. But not from pain in the stump. It's his dreams that make him groan. You know what he's doing in his dreams? He's working again on the railway line to Graaff-Reinet in the olden days. It's the hard work that makes him groan, he says. Other times it's the pain. I can't tell the difference. I've tried to guess. How many nights haven't I listened and said, Is that hard work or is it pain? Then in the morning I go in to him and say: You were dreaming again last night, chum. No, he says, . . . the pain in my stump. I never slept a wink. Or when I say: It seemed to hurt last night, Daddy, he looks at me and says, . . . Maybe. I didn't feel it. I dreamed we reached Heuningvlei. We're living in tents on the side of the line at Heuningvlei.

[*Pause.*]

You asked if he's grey. I had a good look at him. Yes, he's gone grey, but. . . .

HESTER. That's what I said.

JOHNNIE. BUT . . . it suits him. In fact he's looking handsome these days. Don't you believe me?

HESTER. I didn't say that.

JOHNNIE [*watching Hester closely*]. Suppose I were to tell you he's grown a moustache. A smart little Errol Flynn moustache.

HESTER. Good luck to him.

JOHNNIE. And a beard! A voortrekker beard to go with it. And he's getting fat . . . plump!

HESTER. So who cares?

JOHNNIE. You believe me?

HESTER. If you say so.

JOHNNIE. No. He still shaves. Tries to. Cuts himself. Misses little patches where the hairs grow longer and longer until I have to fetch the scissors. He's thin. Skin and bone. He won't eat. I try all sorts of delicacies. Sardines on toast. Warm buttered toast with the silver little fishes. . . .

HESTER. Does he ask about me?

JOHNNIE. No.

HESTER. But he remembers me.

JOHNNIE. I don't know.

HESTER. So then how can you say he still hates me?

JOHNNIE. Because he doesn't speak about you.

HESTER. Maybe he's thinking about me.

JOHNNIE. When you left he said, 'We won't speak about her any more.' You weren't a real Afrikaner by nature, he said. Must be some English blood somewhere, on Mommie's side. He hated you then. He doesn't dream about you. Only the railway line in the old days, the bad old days.

HESTER. Well, just remember that in the eyes of the law it doesn't mean a thing. Just because he doesn't remember or isn't thinking about me doesn't mean a damned thing.

JOHNNIE. Who says it does?

HESTER. Exactly? So when the time comes I want you to be a witness to what you just said.

JOHNNIE. What time?

HESTER. Don't panic. Nothing's happened yet.

JOHNNIE. What's going to happen? I don't like the sound of this. You want something, Hester. You're scheming. You've come back because you want something.

HESTER. I'm saying nothing. I'm passing through and my name is Hester Smit.

JOHNNIE. I know you.

HESTER. No you don't. None of you know me.

JOHNNIE. That's what you used to say.

HESTER. I'll say it again: None of you know me!

JOHNNIE. Just like that, and then there was trouble. None of you know me and you took that job in the café that nearly gave him the stroke, and stayed out late and brought those soldiers home. None of you know me, and you was gone for a week. None of you know me and you went for good. What is it this time? Why have you come back?

HESTER. Must I have a reason to visit my own home?

JOHNNIE. Just leave us alone. We're doing all right.

HESTER. I haven't done anything, for Christ's sake.

JOHNNIE. You're here.

HESTER. Because this is also my home. And him forgetting me doesn't count. She was my mother and he's still my father even if he hates me. So half of everything in here is mine when the time comes.

JOHNNIE. What time is going to come?

HESTER. Something is going to happen some day.

JOHNNIE. Such as what?

HESTER. Such as being dead when your time comes. That happens.

JOHNNIE. The second time.

HESTER. Well, you know what I mean.

JOHNNIE. That's the second time you've said it.

HESTER. You forced me.

JOHNNIE. You're wishing it.

HESTER. I'm not.

JOHNNIE. That's wicked.

HESTER. Dry up, for God's sake.

JOHNNIE. That's sin.

HESTER. It's not Sunday, Dominee.

JOHNNIE [*loudly*]. Wishing for him to die is the wickedest sin in the world!

HESTER. Who's making the noise now?

[*Abrupt silence. Johnnie goes into father's room, returning in a few seconds very nervous and agitated.*]

JOHNNIE. Now you've done it! He's groaning.

HESTER. I've done it?

JOHNNIE. I warned you.

HESTER. Jesus.

JOHNNIE. If there's a stroke you know who's to blame! It looks bad. Wait for the worst, pray for the best.

HESTER. How the hell do you like that!

[*Johnnie now busies himself with the bottle of medicine; a lot of movement in and out of the light to clean the glass, fetch the spoon, measure out the medicine, add water, etc., etc.*]

Fifteen years gone and one hour back but I done it again! Home sweet home where who did it means Hester done it. 'I didn't do it. She did it!' If I laughed too loud that did it. Have a little cry and that will do it. Sit still and mind your own business but sure as the lavatory stinks that will also do it. Well one day I will. And then God help the lot of you.

JOHNNIE. Will what?

HESTER. *Really* do it.

JOHNNIE. Your worst.

HESTER. Worse!

JOHNNIE. There's a word . . . catastrophe. Calamity. Ruin staring us in the face.

HESTER. That's it! In ruins. The lot of you.

JOHNNIE. Smashed to smithereens.

HESTER. And I'll be happy. It's broken and I'm to blame but I'm happy because this time I'll know I did it. So hello be damned and goodbye for good and go back home.

JOHNNIE. You're a rotten egg. There's one in every dozen.

[*Shouting to father's room.*]

Hold on I'm coming!

[*To Hester.*]

For your sake I hope this works.

[*Exit with medicine. Exhausted by her outburst Hester sinks into a chair . . . her elbows on the table, her forehead resting on her palms. She holds this position in silence for a few seconds.*]

HESTER [*without looking up*]. Home.

[*A few more seconds in silence and without movement and then she lifts her head once to look around the room and then drops it back on to her palms. Johnnie returns from his father's room, but stays some distance away from the table in half light.*]

[*Without looking up.*]

You?

JOHNNIE. Yes.

HESTER. I meant a room.

JOHNNIE. What?

HESTER. When I go back. I said I would go back Home. But this is it, isn't it? I'll go back to a room. I'm not hard up for a home.

JOHNNIE [*still in the shadows*]. Leave me your address. I'll write. Let you know how things. . . .

HESTER [*abruptly*]. There's no address.

JOHNNIE. When you settle down and find a new place.

HESTER. There's no address! No names, no numbers. A room somewhere, in a street somewhere. To Let is always the longest list, and they're all the same. Rent in advance and one week's notice—one week to notice it's walls again and a door with nobody knocking, a table, a bed, a window for your face when there's nothing to do. So many times! Then I started waking in the middle of the night wondering which one it was, which room . . . lie there in the dark not knowing. And later still, who it was. Just like that. Who was it lying there wondering where she was? Who was where? Me. And I'm Hester. But what's that mean? What does Hester Smit mean? So you listen. But men dream about other women. The names they call are not yours. That's all. You don't know the room, you're not in his dream. Where do you belong?

JOHNNIE. So what do you do?

HESTER. Wait. Lie there, let it happen, and wait. For a memory. That's the way it works. A memory comes. Suddenly there's going to be a memory of you, somewhere, some other time. And then you can work it all out again. In the meantime, just wait, listen to the questions and have no answers . . . no danger or pain or anything like that, just something missing, the meaning of your name.

[*Pause.*]

It was always the same memory. I was a little girl and I was lying awake one night. I was in here, the kitchen, sleeping in here because you got the mumps in the other room. Mommie and Daddy are in there . . .

[*Pointing to father's room.*]

. . . the door is open and I can hear them talking.
Compensation, he says. They got to. I've only got one leg and a wife and two children. He was talking about the

accident, the explosion and everything is just compensation, compensation . . . hundreds of pounds!

JOHNNIE [*stepping forward into the light*]. The earth opened up! Just like in the Bible. And the mountain fell down on top of him! I know it by heart.

[*Clears his throat and tells the story in a strong vigorous voice.*]

Two miles the other side of Perseverance. They were relaying a section of the line to Uitenhage. It was as hot as hell, which isn't swearing because that's what Bible says. He had slipped away when the others weren't looking to eat prickly pears. There was a bush on the hill, covered with them, fat and ripe. So he was standing there in the shade sucking a juicy one when one of the men from headquarters—those in the white coats—saw him and started to shout. At first Daddy pretended he didn't see him. But then this man got more excited, shouting and swearing and running towards him. The others had all stopped working and were watching. Daddy said he knew then he was in trouble . . . maybe the prickly pear bush was on private property or something. So he picked up his spade and started to go back. But then the man in the white coat went completely mad, screaming and swearing in English like nothing Daddy had ever heard. The others also were jumping up and down—old Dolf, Van Rooyen, Elsie, the lot—jumping up and down and shouting and waving at him. This is it, he thought, I'm fired. The spade was heavy, it was uphill—because he was so frightened he had turned around and was running away for good—and then with a tremendous roar the earth opened! Right in front of his own eyes it just opened and half a mountain was coming down towards him!

[*Pause.*]

He woke up in hospital minus one leg. Dynamite! It's a hell of a word.

HESTER. Does he still talk about it?

JOHNNIE. It's my favourite of all the stories.

HESTER. And the compensation? What does he say about the compensation? Don't look stupid. He was paid hundreds of pounds compensation.

JOHNNIE. He never . . . he doesn't talk about that.

HESTER. Well, he was! I heard him myself, in here. And not just once. There was a lot of talk those days about compensation, and him saying they got to pay. Hundreds of pounds! Because it wasn't his fault. They didn't tell him there was dynamite.

JOHNNIE. So?

HESTER. So I'm just saying.

JOHNNIE. He must have spent it.

HESTER. Him? Hundreds of pounds? Don't make me laugh. Does this look like hundreds of pounds was spent in our lives?

JOHNNIE. What about food? Rent?

HESTER. No you don't! I worked it out. He still gets his disability grant, doesn't he?

JOHNNIE. Yes.

HESTER. And his pension. Well, you work it out and you'll see it covers household and upkeep and all we ever got out of life in here.

JOHNNIE. So then it's in the bank or a post-office book or something.

HESTER. Maybe—only I don't think it is, you see. Because I thought about that one too. When Mommie died and he had to pay the expenses—the coffin and all that—he didn't go to no bank or post-office, he went in there!

[*Pointing to father's room.*]

I was sitting here with the man from the funeral firm and Daddy went in *there* and came back and paid cash!

JOHNNIE. So?

HESTER. So I'm just saying for Christ's sake.

[*Johnnie moves closer to the table, watching Hester carefully. She is tensed and restless.*]
[*Uncertain of how to put her next question.*]
Tell me . . . is . . . a . . . ?

JOHNNIE [*quickly*]. What?

HESTER. Hold your horses! Hell you're in a hurry. What's it like in there?

JOHNNIE. It was a bad turn, but I think he's pulling around. Wilson's Beef and Iron did the trick. Double dose. Calms the nerves and eases the pain. With water after every. . . .

HESTER. Yes, yes, I know. What I mean is, all that old junk —those boxes, man, and suitcases, all that old junk that was packed away when Mommie died and he wouldn't let us fiddle in.

JOHNNIE. You mean his private possessions.

HESTER. Is it still in there? On the wardrobe and under the bed, you know the way it was.

JOHNNIE. Yes.

[*Johnnie watching Hester carefully. She knows it but works up enough courage to continue.*]

HESTER. You want to know something?

JOHNNIE. NO!

HESTER. It's in one of them. The compensation. I'll take you any bet you like it's hidden in one of those boxes.

JOHNNIE. So that's it.

HESTER [*embarrassed but determined*]. Is it?

JOHNNIE. That's why you've come back! That was in your letter!

HESTER. Since when are you a mind-reader?

JOHNNIE. Tell me I'm wrong.

HESTER. What's that prove? Can you deny it's there? No. Because it is. And I'm entitled to half. What would have happened to my share if he passed away and I hadn't come? You didn't know where I was?

JOHNNIE [*closing his eyes*]. He Is Not. . . .

HESTER. HE IS! Some day. He's got to. Everybody does. Sooner or later. . . .

JOHNNIE. No.

HESTER. Yes.

JOHNNIE. The Wilson's Beef and Iron. . . .

HESTER. Shut up! And wake up. Open your eyes! You said so yourself. Grey, you said. And thin. Your own words. Old age and grey and bad turns. Well, that's knocking at death's door . . . LISTEN! If you don't want a slap in your face just shut up and listen. I'm still alive, you see. Alive. He's passing away but I'm still alive. And I'm his daughter. So half of that compensation is mine. Ask any lawyer you like. It's legal and I'm entitled. What good is it doing in there? He doesn't need it. The disability and pension keep him going. So it's just lying there rotting away. Maybe the mould has got it. It got everything else in this house. Or the cockroaches. And then one day when we find it it's cockrotted and useless. So what then is the use of anything? I want it now. Not next year, or when I'm ready for the rubbish heap like him, but Now! Is that such a sin?

JOHNNIE. Yes! It's his, and he's your father. . . .

HESTER. And you're my brother and I'm his daughter so we must all love each other and live happily ever after! Well I got news for you, brother. I don't. There's no fathers, no brothers, no sisters, or Sunday, or sin. There's nothing. The fairy stories is finished. They died in a hundred Jo'burg rooms. There's man. And I'm a woman. It's as simple as that. You want a sin, well there's one. I *Hoer*. I've *hoer*ed all the brothers and fathers and sons and sweethearts in this world into one thing . . . Man. That's how I live and that's why I don't care. And now I'm here and waiting. Because when he wakes up I'm going in there to tell him I want it. My share.

JOHNNIE. No.

HESTER. You think I'm scared of him?

JOHNNIE. No, I mean yes. You will. But don't. Wait. One minute. Just stay still. . . . Sssssh! Let me think. I'm coming!

[*Hurried exit into father's room. Hester lights a cigarette and waits. After a few seconds Johnnie returns.*]

If you find it, will you go?

HESTER. Only my share. All I'm asking for. . . .

JOHNNIE. If you find it, will you go?

HESTER. Yes.

JOHNNIE. Straight away?

HESTER. Yes.

JOHNNIE. You won't worry him?

108

HESTER. No.

[*Pause.*]

Anything else?

JOHNNIE. You won't come back.

HESTER. This is also my home, you know.

JOHNNIE. I'll make a bargain. You take the money, all of it.
Leave me the home.

HESTER. Fair exchange.

JOHNNIE. Then you won't come back, ever?

HESTER. No. So what do we do?

JOHNNIE. He's sleeping. I'll bring in the boxes. You say it's
in the boxes.

HESTER. Or those old suitcases under the bed. I'm prepared
to bet you anything. . . .

JOHNNIE. I'll bring them in.

[*Exit Johnnie. Hester clears the table and waits. Johnnie returns
with the first box—cardboard and tied up with a piece of flaxen twine
—which he puts on the table. Hester stands to one side watching it.*]

Number one.

[*He starts to untie the string.*]

HESTER [*going to the table*]. I'll do that! You just bring in the
boxes.

[*Johnnie sits down and watches her.*]

You think I'm low, don't you?

JOHNNIE. I didn't say that.

HESTER. But you think it.

JOHNNIE. No.

HESTER. So then what you staring at?

JOHNNIE. How much did they pay you?

HESTER. Who?

JOHNNIE. The men. The ones you . . . you know. Your boy-
friends. What's the tariff of charges?

[*Hester ignores the question. She has untied the twine and is now
opening the box. There is a sheet of brown paper on top.*]

It depends on your age, doesn't it? The older you get, and
so on.

HESTER. Mind your own business.

JOHNNIE. Just asking. I'm interested. There's a few in P.E., you know. Jetty Street. I watch them.

[*The first thing to come out of the box is a woman's dress. Hester smells it.*]

HESTER. Hey!

[*Another smell.*]

My God, Johnnie! Smell!

JOHNNIE. What?

HESTER. It's her.

JOHNNIE. Who?

HESTER. Mommie. Smell, man. It's Mommie's smell.

JOHNNIE [*smelling the dress*]. I can't remember.

HESTER. I'm telling you, it's her. I remember. How do you like that, hey? All these years. Hell, man, it hurts. Look, I claim this too. You don't need it. I'll put it on one side and pack it in with my things when I go. Remind me.

[*Back to the box.*]

JOHNNIE [*watching her again*]. Were there many? Hester! On an average, how many times a week?

[*Hester ignores him.*]

I've often wondered, when I see them in Jetty Street. It's illegal of course. You know that.

HESTER [*another dress out of the box—this time a young girl's*]. And this! Jesus, Johnnie. Look.

JOHNNIE. Ribbons.

HESTER. Me, man. Don't you remember? On Sundays? NO!

[*She puts the dress back hurriedly into the box and walks away— sudden fear.*]

JOHNNIE. And now?

HESTER. I've got a funny feeling.

JOHNNIE. What about the money?

[*After a silent struggle Hester goes back to the box and resumes her unpacking. Johnnie watches her.*]

HESTER. Bring in the others.

ACT TWO

The same, about an hour later.

Three or four suitcases and the same number of boxes—all opened —clutter the stage, their contents spilling out on to the floor, gathered together in piles, etc., etc.

Hester is sitting on a suitcase, a photo album open on her lap. She is studying a loose photo in her hands. Johnnie stands to one side holding another, as yet unopened box from his father's room.

A pair of crutches are leaning against a chair.

JOHNNIE. What about that Jansen girl? What was it? Gertrude! Gertrude Jansen!

[*Hester, still studying the photo, shakes her head.*]

She married a De Villiers.

HESTER. Give me some other names.

JOHNNIE. Bet you anything you like it's Gertrude.

HESTER. I said no. Now come on. Who were the others?

JOHNNIE. Let me see, sayeth the blind man. I'll give it to you in alphabetic order. A. Abel. The Abel boys. Ronnie and Dennis. No good. B. Blank. C . . . C. D. . . .

HESTER. Her brother worked at G.M.

JOHNNIE. I've got it. Carrol. Jessie Carrol.

HESTER. That's the one!

JOHNNIE. Jessica Carrol.

[*Places the box beside Hester and studies the photo over her shoulder.*]

Yes, that's her.

HESTER. She hated me.

JOHNNIE. Doesn't look like it.

HESTER. She hated my guts.

JOHNNIE. Got her arm through yours. Smiling. You too.

HESTER. Because we were having this picture taken! But she hated me all right. That time when I got the job at the Astoria Café—she also tried for it, but they took me. So she hated me more. And Stevie Jackson. He was supposed to be her boy-friend, but when he came home on leave it was me he was always running after and taking to Happy Valley. That's when she started telling everyone I had a price. So I buggered her up.

JOHNNIE. I remember now. Daddy was going to send you to reformatory for fighting in the streets.

HESTER. She started it. Scandalizing my name.

JOHNNIE. Hell of a thought, isn't it? Girls' reformatory! All the tough ones together.

HESTER. Who else was there? Me, her, the Abels, Stevie, Gertrude. There was about ten of us.

JOHNNIE. Magda Swanepoel.

HESTER. Yes.

JOHNNIE. Legransie.

HESTER. The Valley Road gang!

JOHNNIE. That's only eight. Me! Nine. . . .

HESTER. You weren't.

JOHNNIE. Wasn't I?

HESTER. You were too small.

JOHNNIE. I joined in the games.

HESTER. You mean you got in the way. Games! What could you play? Nothing. You were a nuisance. Always hanging around! We cook up an idea for something to do and off we go; and then somebody says: Your little brother is following us, Hester. I look back and there you are, trying to hide behind a lamp-post.

JOHNNIE. You used to throw stones at me.

HESTER. Not really.

JOHNNIE. You did, you know.

HESTER. I mean I never really aimed at you.

JOHNNIE [*persistent in his memory*]. Once or twice. . . .

HESTER. When you wouldn't go back!

JOHNNIE. . . . they came quite close.

HESTER. 'Where you going, Hester?' 'Can I come with, Hester?'

JOHNNIE. Because you were supposed to look after me.

HESTER. Didn't I?

JOHNNIE. Not always.

HESTER. What you complaining about? You're still alive.

JOHNNIE. That's true.

HESTER. You messed up some good times for me, my boy. When I did take you with me, you was always getting tired and crying and then I had to carry you. And when we got back always telling him . . . what we did.

JOHNNIE. He asked me.

HESTER. No, he didn't. You just told him.

JOHNNIE. Only to make him happy!

HESTER. By getting me in trouble.

JOHNNIE. NO! By telling him the truth. I just wanted to make him happy by telling him the truth. There was nothing else to tell the truth about. After you went there was nothing left. So many times he said: You always used to tell me the truth, Johnnie. I tried to explain. Hester's gone. There's nothing else, Daddy.

HESTER. You and him! There's a picture somewhere here, of him holding you . . . in the backyard.

[*She is paging through the album.*]

JOHNNIE [*moving away*]. I don't want to see!

HESTER. What's the matter with you? Here it is.

[*She studies the photo. Johnnie watches her.*]

JOHNNIE. Describe it.

HESTER. You're crying, and he's not smiling.

JOHNNIE. More.

HESTER. The backyard—just next to the door. . . .

[*Examining it closely.*]

If you look hard you can just see. . . .

JOHNNIE. Him! Daddy!

HESTER. His crutches.

JOHNNIE. Yes.

HESTER. The way he used to lean on them—sort of forward, but his head up, looking up. . . .

JOHNNIE. That's right.

HESTER. Not smiling. It looks like Sunday. What's the bet it was Sunday? He's got his suit on.

JOHNNIE [*turning to the crutches*]. I forgot all about these.

HESTER [*paging through the album*]. Look at them. What a mob!
[*Examining another one closely.*]

Frikkie! Frikkie Who? Relatives, I suppose.

JOHNNIE. Can you believe it? I forgot all about these being
in there.

HESTER. Is this what we look like? A lot of mistakes? It's
enough to make the dog vomit.
[*Closing the album.*]

Which box did it come from? Doesn't matter.
[*Defeated by the disorder around her, she puts the album aside
negligently.*]

So what's going on?

JOHNNIE. There's another one next to you.

HESTER [*pointing*]. We been through that one?

JOHNNIE. Yes. Those old curtains.

HESTER [*pointing to the new box*]. Well, it better be in here.
[*This box is also tied with string.*]

Where's that knife?

JOHNNIE [*pointing to the crutches*]. I put them on top of the
wardrobe after he had that fall—he said his walking days
were over—and then I forgot all about them.

HESTER. What?

JOHNNIE. These. The crutches.

HESTER [*She can't find the knife and is trying to break the string with
her hands*]. Doesn't he use them any more?
[*Pause. Johnnie stares at her.*]

I asked doesn't he use them any more!

JOHNNIE. Sssssssh! I thought I heard a groan. No. I carry him.
When I sweep the room I carry him in here. He's not heavy.

HESTER. Where's that knife? This looks good, man. It's tied
up tight. Maybe it's in here!

JOHNNIE. It wasn't heavy.

HESTER. That doesn't mean a thing. It would be bank-notes.
Come on, use your muscles.

JOHNNIE. You promised you would go, remember.

HESTER. Yes, yes. Hurry up.

[*The box is opened. Johnnie looks in past Hester's greedy hands.*]

JOHNNIE. Shoes!

[*Hester burrows through a collection of old shoes—men's, women's, and children's. From the bottom of the box she brings out a paper bag which she tears open. The contents spill on to the floor. Johnnie retrieves one.*]

Crutch-rubbers. Shoes and crutch-rubbers. Do you get it? Footwear! Amazing!

[*After a final scrabble through the box, Hester sits down wearily on the suitcase.*]

HESTER. What's the time? No, don't tell me. It doesn't matter.

JOHNNIE [*holding up a pair of girl's shoes*]. Yours?

HESTER. Turn them around. Yes.

JOHNNIE. Dainty. How old? Seven, eight, nine . . . ?

HESTER. Older. Ten or eleven.

[*Johnnie drops them carelessly on the floor.*]

Don't do that! Give here.

[*He passes her the shoes.*]

Yes, one of my birthdays. Mommie bought them, I think. I wore them all that day and after that they were my specials —Sundays and so on—until they pinched so much I couldn't wear them any more.

JOHNNIE. They're still in good shape.

HESTER. So what good was it saving them up for best? What's the use of them now? I wanted them then, when they fitted, when the other girls were laughing at my old ones and my father's socks. The second-hand Smits of Valley Road. That was us! You in my vests, me in his socks, Mommie in his old shoes because the best went into boxes, the boxes into cupboards, and then the door was locked. 'One day you'll thank me,' she used to say. *Ai*, Mommie! You were wrong. There should have been more.

JOHNNIE. More what?

HESTER. Anything. Everything. There wasn't enough of anything except hard times.

JOHNNIE. Because we were hard up. Breadwinner out of action.

HESTER. Other people are also poor but they don't live like we did. Look at the Abels—with only an *Ouma*!

[*Shoes in her hands.*]

Even the birthdays were buggered up by a present you didn't want, and didn't get anyway because it had to be saved. For the rainy day! I've hated rain all my life. The terrible to-morrow—when we're broke, when we're hungry, when we're cold, when we're sick. Why the hell did we go on living?

JOHNNIE [*leaving the box*]. This is fascinating. Let's test your powers of observation.

[*He puts three men's shoes on the floor in front of Hester.*]

HESTER. So?

JOHNNIE. Notice anything strange?

HESTER. I didn't come here to play games.

JOHNNIE. I spotted it. They're all left shoes. They're Daddy's. That's the leg he lost in the explosion!

[*Hester pushes the shoes away with her foot.*]

That's not a very nice thing to do.

HESTER. Run and tell him I did it. Go on . . . Run! Waste my time with rubbish.

[*Looking around.*]

That's what this is. Second-hand rubbish. What's it good for?

[*Johnnie is back on the crutches, examining them, tentatively trying one and then the other. He takes two crutch-rubbers out of his pocket and starts to put them on.*]

JOHNNIE. Our inheritance.

HESTER. All I'm inheriting tonight is bad memories. Makes me sick just to look at it. Can't we pack some away?

[*Hester scoops up an armful and goes around looking for an empty box, but can't find one.*]

JOHNNIE. I can't say I'm bored. Some interesting things are coming to light.

[*The crutch-rubbers are on.*]

There! Good as new.

HESTER [*pointing to a box*]. You quite sure we been through all this? Carefully? I can't remember these hats.

JOHNNIE. You should know. You said you would search the boxes.

HESTER. But you're supposed to tell me when you bring in a new one.

[*Drops the armful she is carrying for a greedy scrabble through the box—hats come out.*]

JOHNNIE. I can't get over this. These crutches. . . .

HESTER. Leave them alone. They're getting on my nerves.

JOHNNIE. But they're comfortable. I used to think they hurt, it looked so sore.

HESTER. I saw enough of them in the old days.

JOHNNIE. Remember his fear of banana-skins? How he used to stand at the window and watch the traffic in the street?

HESTER. Spying on us!

JOHNNIE. Hours on end. But no wonder. I could. It's like being propped up.

HESTER. Soon as I did something . . . Hester! I'm watching you! And there he was peeping behind the curtains.

[*Looks into another box.*]

JOHNNIE. You been through that one.

HESTER. I'm just making sure.

[*Sits.*]

Five hundred pounds is a lot of money.

JOHNNIE. Be the biggest wad I ever seen. Fat as a roll of lavatory paper. What you going to do with it?

HESTER. Plenty.

JOHNNIE. Such as?

HESTER. Such as anything I like. Once you got money you can do anything you like. Change my name! Stay at a posh hotel! I could. And then let them try and refuse to serve me just because I'm sitting by myself in the lounge.

JOHNNIE. What you mean?

[*During Hester's next speech he moves behind her back and there tries out the crutches—a few steps, different positions, opening an imaginary door, etc., etc.*]

HESTER. Some of those big-shot places don't serve you if you're a woman by yourself. I wasn't trying for a pick-up. I just wanted a few beers and a little peace and quiet somewhere nice for a change. They're supposed to be open to the public! But when I walked in they all started staring and then this coolie waiter comes to me and says they don't serve 'ladies' by themselves. Well, this time they will. Because I'll be a boarder. I'll pay in advance. And then let one of those bitches smile as though she's not also selling what she's got between her legs. Give them a chance to say Yes and I DO —because who the hell ever says no—put a ring on their finger and they think they're better! That being married gives them a licence to do it! I'm sick of that lot with their husbands and fashions and happy families. They don't fool me. And I'll tell them. Happy families is fat men crawling on to frightened women. And when you've had enough he doesn't stop, 'lady'. I've washed more of your husbands out of me than ever gave you babies.

JOHNNIE. That's known as exposing your dirty linen in a place of public entertainment.

HESTER. Who the hell do they think they are? Laughing at us like we're a dirty joke or something. Let them live in a back-room where the lavatory is blocked again and the drain is crawling with cockroaches and see if they go on smelling like the soap counter in Woolworth's. Money, brother. Money! You can do anything with money. And my turn is coming. Bring in the boxes. I've wasted enough time.

[*Johnnie leans the crutches against a chair and exits into father's room. Hester moves with a new resolution—clearing a space around her for the next boxes. Johnnie returns with one.*]

JOHNNIE. Light as a feather.

HESTER. Get the others! And put them down here. I don't want them mixed up any more. I mean business now. Soon as I find the money I'm on my way.

[*Johnnie is back with the crutches.*]

And leave those crutches alone for Christ sake.

JOHNNIE. Just—what's the word?—practising.

HESTER. That's mockery.

JOHNNIE. Who?

HESTER. You. You're mocking him.

JOHNNIE. Oh, no.

HESTER. Yes it is. Mockery of a cripple.

JOHNNIE. No, no, no, no.

HESTER. You wait until he catches you.

JOHNNIE. Sssssssh! Keep it down.

[*Exit Johnnie, returning a few seconds later with another load—two bundles of newspapers wrapped up in brown paper and tied with string.*]

HESTER [*still busy with the last box*]. What's all this?

JOHNNIE [*joins her to examine the contents of the box*]. Looks like seeds. Yes. Look here. . . .

[*Pointing to one of the brown paper packets which have come out.*]
. . . Marigolds, Well, I'll be. . . .

[*Taking out other packets.*]
Watermelons, pumpkins, onions . . . beans!

HESTER [*abandoning the box and turning to the bundles*]. And these?

JOHNNIE. Old Mother Earth!

HESTER. Wake up. What's these?

JOHNNIE. Dunno. In the corner next to the wardrobe.

HESTER. Break the strings.

[*Johnnie breaks the string—newspapers spill out. He returns to the seeds.*]
Liewe God!

JOHNNIE. I think they would grow, you know. They've been kept in a cool dry place. All they need now is direct sunlight and Bob's Your Uncle . . . fresh veg.

HESTER. Leave them.

JOHNNIE. But think of it. Ripe watermelons!

HESTER. Get the other boxes.

[*A last scrabble through the pile of newspapers—she picks up one.*]
1937. Six years old. You weren't even born yet.

JOHNNIE. Let's see. 'Roosevelt refuses. . . .'

HESTER [*tearing the paper out of his hands*]. If you don't get those boxes I'll go in there myself!

JOHNNIE. Don't move. I'm on my way.

[*Exit into father's room.*]

[*Hester tries to push back the second flood of rubbish. Johnnie returns with two boxes, puts them down, and exits again. Hester opens these two boxes to find old clothes. She is still busy with them when Johnnie returns with yet another.*]

JOHNNIE. Here's one. Heavy as lead. And listen!

[*He shakes it—Hester abandons the boxes she is busy with and turns feverishly on the new one. It contains packets of old nails, screws, a few tools, a brass door-handle, old keys, etc., etc.*]

Hardware! They thought of everything.

HESTER. More junk. Ten bob on the sale.

JOHNNIE [*holding up a hammer*]. You couldn't buy a ball-pane like this today for love or money.

HESTER. Ten bob on the sale—if you're lucky!

[*She returns to the two half-empty boxes. Johnnie goes through the papers on the floor.*]

[*Holding up a badly torn but clean white shirt.*]

Look at this!

JOHNNIE. 'Chamberlain refuses German offer!' January 1937:

HESTER. A kaffir wouldn't polish the floor with it.

JOHNNIE [*looking at another headline*]. . . . .

HESTER. Other people would have chucked it away.

JOHNNIE. Thirty-six. December 1936.

[*He starts examining the dates on all the papers.*]

HESTER. But we kept it. The Smits of Valley Road washed it, ironed it, folded it up, and packed it away.

JOHNNIE. November 1936. Nearer!

HESTER. Nearer what?

JOHNNIE. 1931, or '30 or '32. Don't you remember? The Bad Years.* 1931 onwards. When he worked on the line to Graaff-Reinet. You remember, man. Daddy. He was always telling us. Something terrible had happened somewhere and it was

Bad Times . . . no jobs, no money. That's what he dreams about now.

The kaffirs sit and watch them work. The white men are hungry. Everybody is greedy. Specially about work—more greedy even than with food. Because work is food—not just today but tomorrow is work. So men look at another man's work the way they used to look at his wife. And those that got it work until the blisters burst and their backs break. He queued for a week to get the job—laying sleepers. Last week ten of his friends was fired. So you work like devils. *They got to see you work!*

And all the time the kaffirs sit and watch the white man doing kaffir work—hungry for the work. They are dying by the dozen!

And then one day in the kloof the other side of Heuningvlei he thought the end had come. His back was hurting like never before, his blisters were running blood. So he cried in the wilderness. 'Why hast thou forsaken me, Lord?' Like Moses. 'Why hast thou forsaken thy lamb?' But it wasn't the end.

That night the railway doctor came to the tents with embrocation and bandages—and he carried on. One mile a day. Heuningvlei, Boesmanspoort, Tierberg, Potterstop. . . . He knows them all! And when they reached Graaff-Reinet the Lord's purpose in all suffering was revealed. Because there he met Mommie.

'I was there in the wilderness—like Moses. The sleepers bent my back, the Lord bent my spirit. But I was not broken. It took dynamite to do that!' Hey?

HESTER. Don't make me sick.

JOHNNIE [*attempting another quote*]. 'And God said unto Moses. . . .'

HESTER. Dry up! I've heard it all. Moses said this, and Abraham said that, and Jesus says something else. Sunday School is over. I'm not a kid any more. Get the other boxes.

JOHNNIE [*collecting the newspapers together*]. In a jiffy.

HESTER. What you doing with those?

JOHNNIE. You might not know it but this is history.

HESTER. Chuck them out.

JOHNNIE. I'd like to read them. When you're gone and life settles down again. There's enough here for. . . .

HESTER. You're as bad as them. It's rubbish.

JOHNNIE. That doesn't stop it from being interesting.

HESTER. I'll chuck them out.

JOHNNIE. No, you won't.

HESTER. Who's going to stop me?

JOHNNIE. Hester!

HESTER. You and who? Him?

JOHNNIE. Hester, if you start something and he wakes up and has a stroke . . . God help you.

HESTER. Here we go again. God help you. God help us. No chance of that, my boy. He never gave a damn about what happened in this house.

JOHNNIE. That sort of talk is not for my ears. I'll get the boxes. [*Exit.*]

HESTER. And I don't blame him! Look at it. Who the hell would have wanted anything to do with us? We weren't just poor. It was something worse. Second-hand! Life in here was second-hand . . . used up and old before we even got it. Nothing ever reached us new. Even the days felt like the whole world had lived them out before they reached us.

[*Johnnie reappears empty-handed.*]

JOHNNIE. Hester.

HESTER. Where's the box?

[*Exit Johnnie.*]

Why the hell did I ever come back?

[*Johnnie reappears, a box in his hand, but he doesn't hand it over immediately.*]

JOHNNIE. Hester.

HESTER. Wasn't there one thing worth saving from all those years?

JOHNNIE. Hester!

HESTER. I'm not talking loud.

JOHNNIE. What will you do if you don't find it?

HESTER. I don't know. I don't even know what it is yet. Just one thing that's got a good memory. I think and think. I try to remember. There must have been something that made me happy. All those years. Just once. Happy.

JOHNNIE. No, I mean the money. The compensation. What will you do if you don't. . . .

[*Pause.*]

Have you . . . ? Yes, you have, haven't you?

[*Hester looks with bewilderment at the chaos around her.*]

You've forgotten what you're looking for!

HESTER. Shut up!

[*She moves among the boxes with growing desperation.*]

You think I've missed it? How long have I been . . . ? Which one did you bring in last? Are you deaf? When did this one come in?

JOHNNIE. I don't know. I've just been fetching. You . . . you said you would. . . .

[*Hester scratches around on the edge of panic.*]

What will you do if you don't . . . ?

HESTER. Something that will make you regret the day you were born.

JOHNNIE [*closing his eyes*]. Dear God, please let Hester find the money!

[*Opening his eyes.*]

Any luck?

HESTER. Get the other!

[*She takes the box from his hand and when he doesn't move immediately gives him a violent shove.*]

Move!

[*Exit Johnnie. As soon as he is out of the room, Hester collapses into a chair, placing the box on the floor at her feet. She stares at it without seeing it—a few seconds of complete vacancy. Then gradually we feel the box intrude itself into her consciousness, challenging her. Without any of the panic of a few seconds previously she opens it and starts to work methodically through its contents. Near the top she finds a bundle of papers.*
Johnnie returns—he is tensed and watches Hester in silence for a few seconds.]

JOHNNIE. All those in favour of sleep hold up their hands!

[*Hester is busy with the papers and ignores him.*]

Hester!

HESTER. What?

JOHNNIE. Bedtime.

HESTER. No.

JOHNNIE. Nothing's going to run away. Tell you what. . . .

HESTER. I said no! Now shut up! Sleep. In here? I'd rather pay a penny and sit all night in a public lavatory. Bring in the other boxes.

[*Goes back to the papers. Johnnie sees the crutches and goes on to them.*]

Documents.

JOHNNIE. I've got something to tell you.

HESTER [*looking at the papers*]. Somebody was born, somebody was baptized, somebody was something else . . . married. . . .

[*Retrieves the paper just discarded.*]

Them. Mommie and Daddy. 1931. Graaff-Reinet. Johannes Cornelius Smit. Anna Van Rooyen.

JOHNNIE. Happily married, faithfully parted by death.

HESTER. Since when?

JOHNNIE. 1931 onwards. Through the years, the setbacks, the hardships. . . .

HESTER. Since when was it happily married?

JOHNNIE. Daddy. He told me. . . .

HESTER. Then tell him from me he's a liar.

JOHNNIE. I've always believed it.

HESTER. Well, you're wrong. What did you know about her? You wasn't even five years when she died.

JOHNNIE. That's true. I've no memories.

HESTER. And I've got plenty. So don't talk to me about happily married.

JOHNNIE. What was she like?

HESTER. See for yourself. There's a picture in the album— it's here somewhere. Smallish. None of her things fitted me when I was big. Always working—working, working, working. . . .

124

[*Pause.*]

Frightened. She worked harder than anybody I ever seen in my life, because she was frightened. He frightened her. She said I frightened her. Our fights frightened her. She died frightened of being dead.

[*She sees Johnnie staring at her.*]

I saw her face in the coffin.

JOHNNIE. You what?

HESTER. Saw her, in the coffin.

JOHNNIE. You peeped?

HESTER. They gave you a last look.

[*She is talking with the calculated indifference of someone not sure of their self-control.*]

He was there. Some uncles and aunties.

JOHNNIE. Where was I?

HESTER. Somewhere else. You were too young.

They pushed me forward. 'Say goodbye to your Mommie, Hester.' I said it—but I couldn't cry. I was dry and hot inside. Ashamed! Of us. Of her, Mommie, for being dead and causing all the fuss. Of him, Daddy, his face cracked like one of our old plates, saying things he never said when she was alive.

And all the uncles and aunties kissing him and patting him on the back and saying 'Shame!' every time they saw you. It was those cousins of his from Despatch, who never ever came to visit us. The whole mob of them, all in black, the little girls in pretty dresses, looking at everything in the house, and us looking like poor whites because there wasn't enough cups to give everybody coffee at the same time. I hated it! I hated Mommie for being dead. I couldn't cry. I cried later. I don't know, maybe two days. Everything was over, the relatives gone. He was in bed with shock. The house was quiet like never before.

Then there was a knock at the back door. I opened it and it was that coolie who always sold the vegetables. 'Where's your Mommie?' he asked. I couldn't say anything at first. 'Girlie, where's your Mommie?' Then I told him. 'Dead.' I just said, 'Dead,' and started to cry. He took off his hat and stood there watching me until I shouted, '*Voetsek!*' and chased him away—and sat down and cried and cried. Because suddenly I knew she was dead, and what it meant, being dead. It's goodbye for keeps. She was gone for ever. So I cried. There was something I wanted to do, but it was too late.

JOHNNIE. What did you want to do?

HESTER. Nothing.

[*Looking at the certificate in her hand.*]

Johannes Cornelius Smit—Anna Van Rooyen. Biggest mistake she ever made!

JOHNNIE. You don't know what you're saying.

HESTER. Yes, I do! I'm saying this was the biggest mistake she ever made. Marriage! One man's slave all your life, slog away until you're in your grave. For what? Happiness in Heaven? I seen them—Ma and the others like her, with more kids than they can count, and no money; bruises every pay-day because he comes home drunk or another one in the belly because he was so drunk he didn't know it was his old wife and got into bed!

JOHNNIE. Daddy never beat Mommie. He was never drunk.

HESTER. Because he couldn't. He was a crock. But he did it other ways. She fell into her grave the way they all do—tired, *moeg.* Frightened! I saw her.

JOHNNIE. This is terrible, Hester.

HESTER. You're damned right it is. It's hell. They live in hell, but they're too frightened to do anything about it because there's always somebody around shouting God and Judgement.

Mommie should have taken what she wanted and then kicked him out.

JOHNNIE. And the children.

HESTER. So what! If you get them you get them and if you don't want them there's ways.

JOHNNIE. Hester! Hester!

HESTER. Hester, Hester what? Hester who? Hester Smit! That's me. I've done it. And I don't care a damn. Two months old and I got rid of it.

JOHNNIE. When the time comes to face your maker. . . .

HESTER. THIS is my time. Now! And no man is going to bugger it up for me the way he did for Mommie.

JOHNNIE. You can be grateful Mommie didn't think like you.

HESTER. Look, there's a couple of words I hate and grateful is one of them.

JOHNNIE. Suppose she had done what you did, and it was YOU. You wouldn't be here now.

HESTER. So I'm here because she was a fool. We're all somebody else's mistake. You. Him too. This. The whole damned thing is a mistake. The sooner they blow it up with their atom bombs the better.

JOHNNIE. You'd like that!

HESTER. Yes.

JOHNNIE. The end of the world.

HESTER. Couldn't care less.

JOHNNIE. If it really had to happen. . . .

HESTER. I'd die laughing. At the look on your faces.

JOHNNIE. Nothing . . . nothing matters?

HESTER. Such as what? Find it.

[*Pointing to the chaos around her.*]

One thing. Marriage?

[*She crumples up the certificate in her hand and throws it away.*]

Being born? Being dead? They're mistakes. All we unpacked here tonight is mistakes.

JOHNNIE. Hester.

HESTER. And the sooner somebody rubs it out the better.

JOHNNIE. Hester, wait.

HESTER. What?

JOHNNIE. I dare you . . . I dare you to commit suicide. Now!

[*She stares at him.*]

JOHNNIE. You said nothing matters. Prove it. I dare you!

HESTER [*statement of fact*]. You dare me.

JOHNNIE. Yes.

127

HESTER. *Ja*, that's right.

JOHNNIE. You will?

HESTER [*ignoring his question*]. You were always daring me. You used to find it—the thing you were too scared to do, and dare me, and watch while I did it and got into trouble. That's what you want, hey? You and him. 'Hester's in trouble again, Pa!'

JOHNNIE. You won't?

HESTER. No.

[*She goes back to the papers.*]

JOHNNIE [*to himself*]. Too much to hope for.

HESTER. You won't get rid of me that easily.

JOHNNIE. But I tried. Whatever happens nobody can say I didn't try. Be brave.

HESTER [*reading from one of the papers*]. 'Johannes Albertus Smit.' That's you.

JOHNNIE. Yes, in full. What's it say?

HESTER [*scanning the letter*]. 'Your application. . . .' The Kroonstad Railway School. From the Principal. Saying they accept your application to be a learner-stoker. And a second-class voucher to get there. November, 1958.

JOHNNIE. Too late now.

HESTER. But you said you tore up your application.

JOHNNIE. That's right.

HESTER. Because you didn't want to go.

JOHNNIE. So?

HESTER. So here he says he *got* your application.

JOHNNIE. These things happen.

[*Pause. Hester thinks about this.*]

HESTER. No. No, they don't. He wouldn't tell you to come if you didn't have asked him if you could come.

JOHNNIE. Where does that get us?

HESTER. You *did* post that application.

JOHNNIE. I see.

HESTER. But you told me you didn't.

128

JOHNNIE. All right I made a mistake. I forgot. I applied. Satisfied?

HESTER. You didn't forget. You lied to me. You know you posted it.

JOHNNIE. I'm telling you I forgot.

HESTER. You knew they said you must come.

JOHNNIE. Can't I forget things too?

HESTER. And you wanted to go!

JOHNNIE. Maybe . . . it's a long time ago . . . ten years . . . my memory. . . .

HESTER. Don't try to get out of it.

JOHNNIE [*desperate*]. What do you want me to say?

HESTER. What are you trying to hide?

JOHNNIE. Nothing. So leave me alone. Understand? Just leave us alone. Take what you want and go!

[*He is squirming—then a clumsy move and the crutches fall—he stands on his feet.*]

Look, what you've made me do!!

[*Pause.*]

Yes, I wanted to go.

They are the most beautiful things in the world! Black, and hot, hissing, and the red glow of their furnaces, their whistles blowing out like ribbons in the wind! And the engine driver, grade one, and his stoker up there, leaning out of the cab, watching the world like kings!

Yes, I wanted to go.

I could have gone. It was up to me. He didn't say anything to stop me posting the forms in duplicate. And when I got the letter saying I must come he even said he was happy because now his son would also work for the railways. I said I'd come home for all my holidays to be with him and give the house a good sweep out. And when I was packing my suitcase he gave me one of his railway shirts—even made a joke, with tears in his eyes—said it would fit when my muscles were big. So there we stood with tears in our eyes, him on his crutches—me with my suitcase. He came to the door and waved to me all the way down Valley Road.

[*Pause.*]

I got as far as the bridge. Nine o'clock in the morning, sun shining, the world a hustle and a bustle, everybody busy, happy—only him, back there. . . .

So, back there. Simple as that. Here. I told him I missed the train. We agreed it was God's will being done. He helped me unpack. Said I could still keep the shirt.

[*Pause.*]

He's not to blame. He was no problem. What he wants, or God wants, I can do. I fetch, I cook, I sweep, I wash, I wait . . . it was ME. What I wanted.

HESTER. What's the matter, Johnnie? Are you scared of hating him?

JOHNNIE. He was my father.

HESTER. He did that to Mommie.

JOHNNIE. She was his wife.

HESTER. Said God and you all felt like sinners. Hate him!

JOHNNIE. How can I hate . . . ?

HESTER. You're frightened of him.

JOHNNIE. Maybe.

HESTER. Yes!

JOHNNIE. All right, yes!

HESTER. You're frightened of hating him!

JOHNNIE. No.

HESTER. You want to hate him.

JOHNNIE. Definitely, no.

HESTER. I hate him! There, I've said it, and I'm still alive. I hate my father.

JOHNNIE. I don't love, I don't hate. I play it safe. I come when called, I go when chased, I laugh when laughed at. . . .

HESTER. Don't make yourself another piece of junk! Hate him! It's clean and new. Let's find something tonight that isn't worn out and second-hand—something bright and sharp and dangerous.

[*Johnnie reacts with terror to this tirade. He picks up the crutches but Hester tries to stop him from going on to them.*]

Don't, Johnnie!

130

JOHNNIE. Let go.

HESTER. No.

JOHNNIE. I feel faint.

HESTER. They're not yours.

JOHNNIE. They fit.

HESTER. Don't you understand? They're his. They're him.

JOHNNIE. I'll ask him for them—tomorrow—when you're gone—I'll tell him. . . .

HESTER. Are you mad?

JOHNNIE. He doesn't need them. I carry him. . . .

HESTER. YOU don't need them!

JOHNNIE [anguish]. I NEED SOMETHING! LOOK AT ME!

[Hester lets go of them and Johnnie goes on to them with feverish intensity.]

Aina! Aina!

HESTER. Then take them. Be cripple!

JOHNNIE. God's will be done. . . .

HESTER. You already look like him. . . .

JOHNNIE. . . . in hell as in heaven. . . .

HESTER. . . . and sound like him. . . .

JOHNNIE. I am his son. He is my father. Flesh of his flesh.

HESTER. That's right. Lick his arse, crawl right up it until your feet hang out. Be HIM.

JOHNNIE. God forgive. . . .

HESTER. That's what you want, isn't it?

JOHNNIE. God forgive you for what you are saying.

HESTER. THERE IS NO GOD! THERE NEVER WAS!

We've unpacked our life, Johannes Cornelius Smit, the years in Valley Road, and there is no God. Nothing but rubbish. In this house there was nothing but useless . . .

[Amok among the contents of the boxes—picking up and throwing about whatever she can get her hands on.]

. . . second-hand poor-white junk!

[Realizes too late that she has just hurled her mother's dress to the floor.]

131

No, no! Look what I've done. Why didn't you stop me?

[*She retrieves it.*]

Mommie, not you. I forgot, not you.

[*Smelling it.*]

She's gone. The smell. . . . I can't. . . . It's gone.
Too late again. Just a rag. An empty rag.
That's how it happened. She got lost, among the rubbish.
I forgot she was here—in here, alive, to touch, to talk to, to
love. She was a chance in here to love something. I wanted
to. The hating was hard. Hate! Hate! So much to hate I
forgot she was here.

[*Smelling the dress.*]

What was it? Mothballs and blue soap. Mothballs in the
wardrobe, sixpence blue soap from the Chinaman on the
corner. Washing, always washing. She was clean. I stink,
Mommie. I'm dirty and I stink. All the hardships, the hating.
I couldn't stop hating and it hurts, it hurts.

JOHNNIE. Pain?

HESTER. It hurts.

JOHNNIE. Home ground!

HESTER. It hurts.

JOHNNIE. An ache or a throb?

HESTER [*intoning non-stop*]. Aina aina aina. . . .

JOHNNIE [*hobbling around on the crutches*]. Wilson's Beef and
Iron! Double dose! Kill or cure! Hold your nose! Open your
mouth! Down the hatch. . . .

[*He gets a spoonful into Hester's mouth. She spits it out violently and
coughs. Johnnie slaps her on the back.*]

Cough it up! Get it off your chest.

HESTER [*pushing him away*]. What's going on?

JOHNNIE. Double dose down the wrong pipe.

HESTER. Shut up!

[*Pause.*]

Here and now!

JOHNNIE. This? This is . . . was . . . will be for ever and ever.
-. . . Let us pray: Oh Lord . . . something . . . our daily bread,

brown bread, the broken loaf and Amen. Grace at supper.
By the grace of God, you me and him in the light of the
lamp with our heads bowed at supper.

This . . . is our home. You've come home. The prodigal
daughter has. . . .

HESTER. The Compensation!

[*Pause.*]

JOHNNIE. That's right. But. . . .

HESTER. Five hundred pounds!

JOHNNIE. According to you.

HESTER. I'll be rich.

JOHNNIE. If you ever find it.

HESTER. So what are we waiting for? Bring in the boxes.

JOHNNIE. There's a catch.

HESTER. Bring in the boxes!!

JOHNNIE. There's none left.

[*Pause.*]

You've had the lot.

HESTER. This . . . ?

JOHNNIE. Is all. The lot. There's nothing left.

HESTER. So where's the money?

JOHNNIE. I tried to warn you.

HESTER. Five hundred pounds. Where is it?

JOHNNIE. I suppose he never got it.

[*Pause.*]

Now you must go. You promised. I'll help you pack.

HESTER. NO!

You've found it.

JOHNNIE. Hester. . . .

HESTER. Let me feel your pockets.

JOHNNIE. You promised you would go.

HESTER. Then he's got it.

JOHNNIE. No.

HESTER. He's awake!

JOHNNIE. NO.

133

HESTER. He knows I'm looking for it and he's hiding it. Go in there and tell him I want it.

JOHNNIE. 'Strue's there's a living God. . . .

HESTER. If you won't I will!

JOHNNIE. That will kill him. He hates the sight of you.

HESTER [*shouting*]. Johannes Cornelius Smit, I want my share!

JOHNNIE. I'm warning you.

[*Exit Hester into father's room.*]

Something's going to happen now. There's dynamite, somewhere in this house. In Hester's heart. The heart that hurts. Was it like this? Did he feel like this? He was running—the others were shouting. I'm standing still, nobody's shouting. . . . 'I was standing still, leaning on my. . . .'

[*Hester returns slowly.*]

Five, four, three, two, one. . . .

HESTER. Where is he?

JOHNNIE. Dead.

HESTER. Dead?

JOHNNIE. Dead as a dud. He died.

[*Hester approaches Johnnie.*]

Gave up the ghost—all the words! . . . called by God, with the singing angels . . . laid to rest. . . .

[*Hester is now in front of Johnnie. She hits him once. He closes his eyes and speaks with bitter violence.*]

The Beef and Iron was a flop! Double dose three times a day! But he died!

[*Hester pulls the crutches out from under his arms. He falls to the ground. She kicks him.*]

More! Explode! Swallow me up. Let the mountain fall! This is the end of the world.

[*Hester goes down on her knees to beat Johnnie with clenched fists— stopping eventually from sheer exhaustion. She gets up and staggers to a chair. Johnnie remains on the floor—he will not move until after Hester's final exit.*]

[*A long pause as the violence ebbs.*]

Don't be fooled. This isn't silence. I can hear you breathing.

Silence isn't what you think it is. Silence is waiting—for it to happen, anything—a noise, or a groan or a call.

Sometimes it wasn't any of them—just the sound of his medicine bottles rattling in the dark in the middle of the night. But I was waiting. I'd go in and see if he was all right. 'Have I got enough?' he'd ask me. So I'd look. 'Yes, chum, you've got enough. Six doses if there's a drop.' 'Even so,' he would say, 'get me another bottle tomorrow—the safe side in case of.'

And sometimes when it was like that, the waiting just stopped, the silence went and there were frogs croaking in the river or a cricket in the yard. Little Happy Noises! And we would talk quietly. One night it was all about modern means of transport and he was saying he could still remember the old ox-wagon days and how long it took to go from Despatch to P.E. . . . Suddenly in the middle of it his face went all sort of puffy! His mouth started shivering, he closed his eyes. I thought it was a stroke! Then I saw he was crying.

'Don't let them cut off my other leg,' he said. 'Promise you won't let them.'

'Don't be silly,' I said. 'Of course they won't. Why would they do a stupid thing like that?' 'But promise me you won't let them if they want to all the same.' 'Over my dead body, chum,' I said. 'Over my dead body.'

I went back to bed.

HESTER. Johnnie.

JOHNNIE [*doesn't hear her*]. I missed the end.

HESTER. Johnnie!

JOHNNIE. He died in my sleep.

HESTER. When?

[*Pause.*]

A long time ago? Yesterday?

JOHNNIE. Something like that.

HESTER. Today?

JOHNNIE. No! The other day.

I woke up on the sofa the other day, just lay there waiting for the first cough or call of the new day. Waited and waited. Started to wonder. Got worried. Went in, 'Rise and Shine!' I said. 'Beef and Iron time, Daddy!'

[*Pause.*]

Nothing.

[*Pause.*]

[*Hester leaves the room quietly, wearily.*]

The room was dark, the curtain still closed. I listened . . .
I didn't want to look!

[*Loud.*]

'Daddy!' I sat on my chair next to his bed.

'Wake up, Lazybones! You'll miss the early worm!' . . . all
our little jokes. I waited and waited . . . it might have been
days . . . called and called till I knew he was dead.

I tried to work it out. 'This is it,' I thought. 'The end.' Of
what? Of him. Of Waiting. Of pain in the other room.

'You're on your own, Johnnie Smit,' I said to myself. 'From
now on it's you—just you and wherever you are—you in the
middle of a moment. The other room is empty.'

[*Hester returns, her coat on, carrying her suitcase. She puts it down
and sits on it.*]

HESTER. I'm on my way.

JOHNNIE. Where.

HESTER. Back. My room. I'm paid up for the month. There's
a week left. She won't even know I'm gone.

JOHNNIE. When's the train leave?

HESTER. Sometime. Ten o'clock.

JOHNNIE. That's right. All stations via Kommodagga.

HESTER. I'll wait at the station. I've had enough of this.

JOHNNIE. There's some bread somewhere . . . butter and jam
. . . make yourself sandwiches. It's a long trip.

HESTER. Get up, Johnnie.

JOHNNIE. I'm just resting.

HESTER. I'm sorry about what happened. I didn't mean it.
But why did you lie to me? Bluff he was in there?

JOHNNIE. I am. . . . [*Pause.*]

HESTER. What?

JOHNNIE. It's hard to describe. It feels like . . . I'm ashamed.
Of me. Of being alone. Just me in my whole life. It was so

different with him. He was in there, something else, somewhere else. Even tonight, just pretending it helped. You believed he was in there, didn't you?

HESTER. Yes.

JOHNNIE. If only his ghost would come back and haunt me! Even if I went grey with fright! Do you believe in ghosts, Hester?

HESTER. Hang on, Johnnie. Listen—pack up and come with me.

JOHNNIE. Where?

HESTER. Jo'burg. Where else?

JOHNNIE. A holiday?

HESTER. Or for good.

JOHNNIE. And then?

HESTER. Anything! Anything's better than this, *Boetie*. Get a job, a girl, have some good times. What do you say?

[*Pause. She realizes it is useless.*]

You won't come.

JOHNNIE. Suppose—just suppose there are ghosts, and he did come back to haunt, and I was gone!
I'll stay. Just in case, I'll wait.

HESTER [*gesture to the chaos on the floor, the house*]. Anyway you can have it. Okay? It's all yours. The house and everything. Tell them I said it's yours.

JOHNNIE. Who?

HESTER. The people. There's always people around when somebody dies. Officials. Tell them I gave you my share. It was my will. Read the newspapers, plant the seeds, have a garden. . . .

JOHNNIE. Don't you need dung?

HESTER. That's it! . . . Live happily. Try, Johnnie, try to be happy.

JOHNNIE. Why? What's this?

HESTER. I don't know. I don't know what it is. But there's something else—something we never had.

JOHNNIE. And you? Any plans?

HESTER. Back like I said. There's always jobs. And I got my room. That's me—a woman in a room. I'm used to it now.

[*Stands and moves upstage to the edge of the light.*]

It's strange, you know. I can see it—see it happening. All of this. I'll walk out of that door, through the streets to the station, sit in the waiting-room. Then the train at ten and all the way back. It's hard. Things are too clear. This, there, Jo'burg tomorrow when I get there. The rooms—the dark rooms, the many faces—and one of them me, Hester Smit. I'm too far away from my life.

I want to get back to it, in it, be it, be me again the way it was when I walked in. It will come, I suppose. But at this moment—there she is waiting, here she is going, and somebody's watching all of it. But it isn't God. It's me.

Goodbye, Johnnie.

[*Exit Hester.*]

[*Johnnie makes a move as if to get up, then sees the crutches some distance away from him on the floor. He stares at them for a few seconds then very laboriously drags himself along the floor to them. With equal effort he holds them upright and goes on to them.*

He stands still, on one leg for a few seconds, then realizes he is standing on the wrong leg and changes over.]

JOHNNIE. Why not? It solves problems. Let's face it—a man on his own two legs is a shaky proposition. She said it was mine. All of it—my inheritance. These, seeds . . . and memories. More than enough!

They can look now. Shine their lights in my face, stare as hard as they like. I've got a reason. I'm a man with a story. 'I was eating prickly pears, Mister, leaning on my spade having a rest, minding my own business, when suddenly the earth opened and the mountain fell on me. . . .'

They'll say 'shame', buy me a beer, help me on buses, stop the traffic when I cross the street . . . slowly. . . .

Yes! Everything slower now. Everything changed. The time it takes. Leave at sunset, arrive in the dark, twilight on the bridge. The shadow on the wall different . . . but me . . . a different me!

What's the word? Birth. Death. Both. Jesus did it in the Bible.
 [*Pause.*]
Resurrection.
 [*Pause.*]

BOESMAN AND LENA

—

Boesman and Lena was first presented in the United States by Theodore Mann and Paul Libin in association with John Berry at Circle in the Square, June 22, 1970, under the direction of John Berry. Set design was by Karl Eigsti, costume design by Margie Goldsmith and lighting design by David F. Segal. The cast was as follows:

BOESMAN .... *James Earl Jones*
LENA .... *Ruby Dee*
OUTA .... *Zakes Mokae*

The play was originally presented at the Rhodes University Little Theatre, Grahamstown, South Africa, July 10, 1969, under the direction of the author and with the following cast:

BOESMAN .... *Athol Fugard*
LENA .... *Yvonne Bryceland*
OUTA .... *Glynn Day*

CHARACTERS

BOESMAN, *a Coloured man*
LENA, *a Coloured woman*
OUTA, *an old African*

ACT ONE

An empty stage.

A Coloured man—Boesman—walks on. Heavily burdened. On his back an old mattress and blanket, a blackened paraffin tin, an apple box . . . these contain a few simple cooking utensils, items of clothing etc., etc. With one hand he is dragging a piece of corrugated iron. Barefoot, shapeless grey trousers rolled up to just below the knee, an old shirt, faded and torn sports-club blazer, cap on his head.

He chooses a spot, then drops the corrugated iron, gets down his load, and slumps to the ground beside it. He has obviously walked very far. He waits.

After a few seconds a Coloured woman—Lena—appears. She is similarly burdened—no mattress though—and carries her load on her head. As a result, she walks with characteristic stiff-necked rigidity. There is a bundle of firewood under one arm. Also barefoot. Wearing one of those sad dresses that reduce the body to an angular, gaunt cipher of poverty.

A life of hardship and dissipation obscures their ages, but they are most probably in their fifties.

Boesman looks up slowly as Lena appears. He watches her with a hard, cruel objectivity. He says nothing. She has been reduced to a dumb, animal-like submission by the weight of her burden and the long walk behind them, and in this condition almost misses him sitting to one side, propped up against his bundle. Realizing she has passed him, she stops, but does not turn to face him in case they have to walk still further.

LENA. Here?

[*Boesman clears his throat and spits. She waits a few seconds longer for a word from him, then turns slowly and joins him. The bundle of firewood falls to the ground. Her arms go up and with the last of her strength she gets her bundle down. Her relief as she does so is almost painful. She sits down slowly. For a few seconds she just rests, her head between her knees, breathing deeply. Then she stretches forward and works a finger between the toes of one of her feet. It comes away with a piece of mud. She looks at it, squashing it between her fingers.*]

Mud! Swartkops!

[*She now looks at the world around her for the first time—she knows*

143

it well—then still higher up, into the sky, searching for something.]
Too late now. [*Pause.*] No. There's one.

[*She is obviously staring up at a bird. Softly . . .*]
Jou moer!

[*She watches it for a few seconds longer, then scrambles to her feet and shakes her fist at it.*]
Jou moer!!

[*Boesman watches her, then the bird, then Lena again. Her eyes follow it as it glides out of sight.*]
So slowly . . . ! Must be a feeling, hey. Even your shadow so heavy you leave it on the ground.

[*She sits down again, even more exhausted now by her outburst. She cleans the mud from between her other toes while she talks.*]
Tomorrow they'll hang up there in the wind and laugh. We'll be in the mud. I hate them.

[*She looks at Boesman.*]
Why did you walk so hard? In a hurry to get here? 'Here', Boesman! What's here? This . . . [*the mud between her fingers*] . . . and tomorrow. And that will be like this! *Vrot!* This piece of world is rotten. Put down your foot and you're in it up to your knee.

That last *skof* was hard. Against the wind. I thought you were never going to stop. Heavier and heavier. Every step. This afternoon heavier than this morning. This time heavier than last time. And there's other times coming. '*Vat jou goed en trek!*' Whiteman says *Voetsek! Eina!*

[*Boesman is watching her with undisguised animosity and disgust.*]
Remember the old times? Quick march! Even run . . . [*a little laugh*] . . . when they chased us. Don't make trouble for us here, Boesman. I can't run any more.
Quiet, hey! Let's have a *dop.*

[*Lena registers Boesman's hard stare. She studies him in return.*]
You're the hell-in. Don't look at me, *ou ding.* Blame the whiteman. Bulldozer!

[*Another laugh.*]
Ja! You were happy this morning. 'Push it over, my *baas!*' '*Dankie, baas!*' '*Weg is ons!*'

It was funny, hey, Boesman! All the *pondoks* flat. The poor people running around trying to save their things. You had a good laugh. And now? Here we sit. Just now it's dark, and Boesman's thinking about another *pondok*. The world feels big when you sit like this. Not even a bush to make it your own size. Now's the time to laugh. This is also funny. Look at us! Boesman and Lena with the sky for a roof again.

[*Pause. . . . Boesman stares at her.*]

What you waiting for?

BOESMAN [*shaking his head as he finally breaks his silence*]. *Yessus*, Lena! I'm telling you, the next time we walk. . . .

LENA. Don't talk about that now, man.

BOESMAN. The Next Time We Walk! . . .

LENA. Where?

BOESMAN. . . . I'll keep on walking. I'll walk and walk. . . .

LENA. *Eina!*

BOESMAN. . . . until you're so bloody *moeg* that when I stop you can't open your mouth!

LENA. It was almost that way today.

BOESMAN. Not a damn! Wasn't long enough. And I knew it. 'When she puts down her bundle, she'll start her rubbish.' You did.

LENA. Rubbish?

BOESMAN. That long *drol* of nonsense that comes out when you open your mouth!

LENA. What have I said? I'm *moeg! Eina!* That's true. And you were happy this morning. That's also true.

BOESMAN. I'm still happy.

LENA. You happy now?

BOESMAN [*aggressively*]. I'm always happy.

LENA [*mirthless laughter, clapping her hands*]. *Ek sê!* His backside in the Swartkops mud, but Boesman's happy. This is a new sort of happy, *ou ding*. The hell-in happy.

BOESMAN. Why shouldn't I be happy?

LENA. *Ja*, that's the way it is. When I want to cry, you want to laugh.

BOESMAN. Cry!

LENA. Something hurt. Wasn't just your fist.

BOESMAN. Snot and tears because the whiteman pushed over a rotten old *pondok*? That will be the day. He did me a favour. I was sick of it. So I laughed.

LENA. And now?

BOESMAN. Yes. You think I can't laugh now?

LENA. Don't be a bastard.

BOESMAN. You want to hear me?

LENA. NO!

BOESMAN. Then shut up, or you will! I'm a happy *Hotnot*. Laughing all the time . . . inside! I haven't stopped since this morning. You were a big joke then, and if you don't watch out you'll be a big joke now.

LENA. Big joke? Because I cried? No, *here*, Boesman! It was too early in the morning to have your life kicked in its *mòer* again. Sitting there in the dust with the pieces . . . *Kaalgat!* That's what it felt like! . . . and thinking of somewhere else again. Put your life on your head and walk, sister.
Another day gone. Other people lived it. We tramped it into the ground. I haven't got so many left, Boesman.

BOESMAN. If your legs worked as hard as your tongue then we were here long ago.

LENA. It's not my fault.

BOESMAN. Then whose? Every few steps . . . 'Rest a bit, Boesman.' 'I'm tired, Boesman.'

LENA. *Arme ou Lena se maer ou bene.*

BOESMAN. You weren't resting.

LENA. I was.

BOESMAN. You lie.

LENA. What was I doing?

BOESMAN. You were looking for that *brak* of yours.

LENA. *Brak?*
   [*She remembers.*] *Hond!*
   Haai! Was it this morning?

BOESMAN. You almost twisted your head off, you were looking

behind you so much. You should have walked backwards today.

LENA. He might have followed me. Dogs smell footsteps.

BOESMAN. Follow you! You fancy yourself, hey.

LENA. Anyway you weren't in such a hurry yourself. You didn't even know where we were going.

BOESMAN. I did.

LENA. Swartkops?

BOESMAN [*emphatically*]. Here! Right here where I am.

LENA. No, Boesman. This time you *lieg*.

BOESMAN. Don't say to me I *lieg*! I'm not mix-up like you. I know what I'm doing.

LENA. Why didn't we come the short way then?

BOESMAN. Short way? Korsten to Swartkops? What you talking about?

LENA. It didn't use to feel so long. That walk never came to an end. I'm still out there, walking!

BOESMAN [*a gesture of defeat*].

It's useless to talk to you.

[*He goes through Lena's bundle and finds two bottles of water. He uncorks one and has a drink. He then starts unpacking his bundle.*]

LENA. All you knew was to load up our things and take the empties to the bottle store. After that . . . !

[*She shakes her head.*]

'Where we going, Boesman?' 'Don't ask questions. Walk!' *Ja*, don't ask questions. Because you didn't know the answers. Where to go, what to do. I remember now. Down this street, up the next one, look down that one, then turn around and go the other way. Not lost? What way takes you past Berry's Corner twice, then back to where you started from? I'm not a fool, Boesman. The roads are crooked enough without you also being in a *dwaal*.

First it looked like Redhouse, or Veeplaas. Then it was Bethelsdorp, or maybe Missionvale. *Sukkel* along! The dogs want to bite but you can't look down. Look ahead, sister. To what? Boesman's back. That's the scenery in my world. You don't know what it's like behind you. Look back one day,

Boesman. It's *me*, that thing you *sleep* along the roads. My life. It felt old today. Sitting there on the pavement when you went inside with the empties. Not just *moeg*. It's been that for a long time. Something else. Something that's been used too long. The old pot that leaks, the blanket that can't even keep the fleas warm. Time to throw it away. How do you do that when it's yourself?

I was still sore where you hit me. Two white children came and looked while I counted the bruises. There's a big one here, hey. . . .

[*Touching a tender spot under one eye.*]

You know what I asked them? 'Does your mother want a girl? Go ask your mother if she wants a girl.' I would have gone, Boesman.

BOESMAN. And then?

LENA. Work for the madam.

[*Boesman laughs derisively.*]

They also laughed, and looked some more, *ja*, look at Lena! *Ou Hotnot meid.* Boesman's her man. Gave her a hiding for dropping the empties. Three bottles broken. Ten cents. Ten cents worth of bruises.

BOESMAN [*indifferently*]. You should have gone.

LENA [*she has to think about it*].

They didn't want me.

BOESMAN [*another laugh, then stops himself abruptly*].

You think *I* want you?

LENA [*she also thinks about this before answering*].

You took me. You came out with the wine, put it in your bundle, then you said 'Come!' and walked. I wanted to say something. The word was in my mouth! But the way you did it . . . no questions, didn't even look at me . . . just picked up and walked. So I followed you. Didn't even know where until I felt the mud between my toes. Then I knew. Swartkops again! Digging for bait. Mudprawns and worms in an old jam tin. A few live ones on top, the dead one at the bottom. 'Sixty cents, my *baas*. Just dug them out!' *Lieg* your soul into hell for enough to live.

How we going to dig? We haven't even got a spade.

BOESMAN. I'll get one.

LENA. *Oppas* they don't get *you. Blourokkie* next time they catch you stealing.

Haai, Boesman! Why here? This place hasn't been good to us. All we've had next to the Modderspruit is hard times. [*A little laugh.*] And wet ones. Remember that night the water came up so high? When we woke up *pap nat* with all our things floating down to the bridge. You got such a *skrik* you ran the wrong way.

[*She laughs at the memory.*]

BOESMAN. I didn't!

LENA. What were you doing in the deep water? Having a wash?

[*Another laugh.*]

It was almost up with you that night. Hey! When was that? Last time?

[*Pause. . . . Lena thinks.*]

Boesman! When was our last time here? I'm talking to you.

[*Boesman deliberately ignores her, and carries on sorting out the contents of his bundle.*]

Boesman!!!

[*Pause. . . . No reaction from him.*]

Don't be like that tonight, man. This is a lonely place. Just us two. Talk to me.

BOESMAN. I've got nothing left to say to you. Talk to yourself.

LENA. I'll go mad.

BOESMAN. What do you mean, 'go' mad? You've been talking to yourself since . . .

[*Pause. . . . Lena waits, he remembers.*]

Ja! . . . since our first walk.

LENA. First walk?

BOESMAN. That night, in the brickfields.

LENA. Coega to Veeplaas!

BOESMAN. First you cried. When you stopped crying, you started talking. I was tired. I wanted to sleep. But you talked. 'Where we going?' 'Let's go back.' Who? What? How?

Yessus! On and on. Then I thought it. 'Boesman, you've made a mistake!'

LENA. Coega to Veeplaas.

BOESMAN. You talked there too. So I thought it again.

LENA. Mistake.

BOESMAN. Mistake. Every time you opened your mouth . . . until I stopped listening.

LENA. I want somebody to listen.

BOESMAN. To what? That *gebabbel* of yours. When you *poep* it makes more sense. You know why? It stinks. Your words are just noise. Nonsense. *Die geraas van 'n vervloekte lewe.* Look at you! Listen to you! You're asking for a lot, Lena. Must I go mad as well?

LENA. I asked you when we came here last. Is that nonsense?

BOESMAN. Yes! What difference does it make? To anything? You're here now!

LENA [*looking around*]. I'm here now.

[*Surge of anger.*] I know I'm here now. Why? Look at it, for God's sake. Is this the best you could do? What was wrong with Veeplaas?

BOESMAN. What's right with it?

LENA. There's other people there! What's the matter with you? Ashamed of yourself?

[*Boesman turns away from her, dragging their one mattress to the spot where he will build the shelter. He then picks up the piece of corrugated iron and examines it, trying it out in various positions . . . as a roof, a wall, etc.*]

LENA. Or Missionvale! Redhouse! There's a chance of a job there on the saltpans.

Not even a dog to look at us. Everytime we come back here it feels like I've never left. Maybe this is the last time here I'm trying to remember. *Haai!*

[*She shakes her head . . . then pauses.*]

Wasn't it after Redhouse? Out last time here. Remember, that *boer* chased us off his land. Then we came here. Is that right?

[*Boesman ignores her.*]

Then we went to Korsten.

BOESMAN. After here we went to Korsten?

LENA. *Ja.* [*Boesman laughs at her derisively.*] How was it then?
[*Pause.*] You won't tell me.

BOESMAN [*putting down the piece of iron*].
Make the fire.

LENA. Let's have a *dop* first. I'm feeling the cold. Please,
Boesman!

[*Without another look at her he walks off. Lena gets stiffly to her
legs and starts to make the fire. A box is positioned to shield it from
the wind, then the bundle of firewood untied, the wood itself broken
into pieces, a piece of paper to get it started, etc.*]

LENA. Walk our legs off for this! Piece of bread and black tea.
No butter . . . not even for bruises.

[*A thought crosses her mind. She straightens up, thinks hard for a
few seconds, then shakes her head.*]

No. [*She looks around.*] Maybe he's right. What's the difference.
I'm here now.
'Here!' After a long life that's a thin slice. No jam on that
one. Or *kondens melk!* There's *soeterigheid* for you. Maybe if
we get lots of prawns. . . .

[*Another thought. . . . She thinks hard. . . .*]

It was after Redhouse. Collecting prickly pears. Then they
found our place there in the bush. *Loop, Hotnot!* So *Hotnot
loops* . . . to Swartkops. Here. The last time here. I was right!
[*Pause.*]

No, we ran! The *boer* had a gun. When he showed us the
bullets Boesman dropped his tin and went down that road
like a rabbit. . . .

[*Laughing . . . her hands to her backside in an imitation of the scene.*]
. . . *Moenie skiet, baas!*

Me too, but the other way. Where did I find him? . . . looking
at the mud, the hell-in because we had lost all our things
again. Just our clothes, and each other. Never lose that. Run
your legs off the other way but at the end of it Boesman
is waiting. How the hell does that happen?
Redhouse—Swartkops! I was right. He must laugh at himself.

[*Back to her chores.*]

And then? Somewhere else! *Ja,* of course. One of them. Veeplaas. Or Missionvale. Maybe Bethelsdorp. Lena knows them all.

[*Pause.*]

But which one . . . that time?

[*She straightens up and looks around.*]

Which way . . . ?

[*Moving around, trying to orientate herself physically.*]

Let me see now. We came. . . . No. Those lights! What's that? Where is . . . it's round all right . . . where the hell is . . . *Yessus!* I'm right in the middle. No wonder I get drunk when I try to work it out. . . .

[*Sudden desperation.*]

Think, man! It happened to you.

[*Closes her eyes in an effort to remember.*]

We were here. Then we left. Off we go. . . . We're walking . . . and walking . . . where we walking? Boesman never tells me. Wait and see. Walking. . . .

Somewhere, his shadow. In front of me. Small man with a long *maer* shadow. It's stretching back to me over the veld because we're walking to the sun and it's going down. . . .

Veeplaas! That's where the sun goes. Behind it there into the bush. So Veeplaas is. . . .

[*Looking now for the sun.*]

Waar die donner is . . . ?

[*Pause.*]

Finished. So what. I got it in here [*pointing to her head*]. Redhouse—Swartkops—Veeplaas!

[*She is very pleased with herself.*]

Get a move on now. I'm nearly here. Redhouse—Swartkops —Veeplaas. . . .

[*She carries on working, laying out mugs, filling a little pot with water, etc. . . . all the time muttering to herself the sequence of places she has established.*]

It's coming! Korsten! Empties, and the dog. *Hond!* How was it now? Redhouse—Swartkops—Veeplaas—Korsten. Then this morning the bulldozers . . . and then. . . .

[*Pause.*] Here! I've got there!

[*She is very happy.*] 'Here', sister. You ran that last bit. Bundle and all.

[*She is humming away happily to herself when Boesman returns with a few odds and ends—an old sack, few pieces of wood, another piece of corrugated iron, an old motor-car door, etc.—out of which he will fashion their shelter for the night. He registers Lena's good humour and watches her suspiciously as he starts to work. Lena realizes this and laughs.*]

Why you looking at me so *skeef*?

[*He says nothing. Lena hums a little song.*]

Remember the times I used to sing for us?

'Da . . . da . . . da. . . .'

BOESMAN. What's the matter with you?

LENA. Feeling fine, darling. I'm warm. You know why? I've been running. You should have seen me! I'm not as old as I thought. All the way from Redhouse. . . .

[*The rest of her sentence is lost in laughter at the expression on his face.*]

. . . and now I'm here. With you.

Da . . . da . . . da. . . .

BOESMAN [*after watching her for a few more seconds*]. Show me the wine!

LENA. Look for yourself.

[*Boesman leaves his work on the shelter. He goes through his bundle and examines two bottles of wine. They are both intact. Lena laughs at him.*]

How's it for a *dop*?

[*He puts away the bottles and goes back to work.*]

Hey, you know what I was thinking just now. *Blikkie kondens melk.* What do you say? If we get lots of prawns. Sugar's not enough, man. I want some real sweetness. Then you can be as *bedonnerd* as you like.

[*She starts singing, shuffling out a few dance steps at the same time.*]

> Ou blikkie kondens melk
> Maak die lewe soet;
> Boesman is 'n Boesman
> Maar hy dra 'n Hotnot hoed.

Look at this! Lena's still got a *vastrap* in her old legs. You want to dance, Boesman? Not too late to learn. I'll teach you.

BOESMAN. Just now you get a bloody good *klap*!

LENA. *Ja!* See what I mean. This time I'm laughing, and you . . . ! *Vies!* You don't like it when somebody else laughs. Well, you laughed at me for nothing. Because I was right! Last time here *was* after Redhouse. You won't mix me up this time. I remember. The *boer* pointed his gun and you were gone, non-stop to Swartkops. Then Veeplaas. Then Korsten. And now here. How's that!

[*She laughs triumphantly. Boesman lets her enjoy herself. He waits for his moment.*]

And I'm not finished. Wait and see. I'm going to think some more. I'll work it out, back and back until I reach Coega Kop. Then I'll have it. Coega Kop to here. So what you got to say?

BOESMAN. Nothing.

LENA [*another laugh*]. Now you're really the hell-in. Nothing to laugh at.

BOESMAN. Nothing to laugh at?

[*He disproves this with a small laugh.*]

LENA. You can't laugh at me.

[*Another laugh from Boesman.*]

I'm right, Boesman!

BOESMAN. How was it? Swartkops after Redhouse?

LENA. Yes!

BOESMAN. And from here we went to . . .

LENA. Korsten!

[*Boesman shakes his head with another laugh.*]

It's no good, Boesman. I know what you're trying. You're not going to do it this time. Go laugh at yourself.

[*She goes back to her work, but there is an edge of something new in her voice as she repeats the sequence with exaggerated emphasis.*]

Redhouse—Swartkops—Veeplaas—Korsten . . . Here! Where I am.

[*She looks up at Boesman, but he pretends total indifference. This adds to her growing uncertainty. She looks around. We see her trying*]

hard to remember, to work it out yet again. Boesman waits. He knows.
Eventually . . .]

Is it wrong?

BOESMAN [*strolling up to the fire to fetch something*].
Why do you stop singing?

LENA. Is it wrong, Boesman?

BOESMAN [*he takes his time, finding whatever he is looking for first before answering*].
What about . . . Swartkops—Veeplaas—Redhouse?

LENA [*vacantly*]. Swartkops . . . Veeplaas. . . .

BOESMAN. Or this. Veeplaas.

LENA. Veeplaas.

BOESMAN. Redhouse . . .

LENA. Redhouse . . .

BOESMAN. Korsten!

LENA. Veeplaas—Redhouse—Korsten? [*Pause.*] Where's Swartkops?

[*The sight of her vacant confusion is too much for Boesman. He has a good laugh, now thoroughly enjoying himself.*]

To hell with it! I'm not listening to you. I'm here!

BOESMAN. Where? Veeplaas?

LENA [*closing her eyes*]. I'm here. I know how I got here. Redhouse, then Swartkops. . . .

[*Pause—she has forgotten.*]

Wait . . . ! Redhouse—Swartkops. . . .

BOESMAN. Go on! But don't forget Bethelsdorp this time. You've been there too. And Missionvale. And Kleinskool.

LENA. Don't mix me up, Boesman!

[*Trying desperately to remember her sequence.*]

Redhouse—Swartkops . . . then Veeplaas . . . then. . . .

BOESMAN. It's wrong!

[*Pause . . . she looks at him desperately. He leaves his work on the shelter and goes to her.*]

Yes! It's wrong! Now what you going to do?

LENA [*she moves around helplessly, trying to orientate herself physically*].

It's mixed up again. I had it!

BOESMAN. Look at you! *Babalas!* . . . from yesterday's wine. Yesterday you were drunk. One or the other. Your whole life.

LENA [*staring off in a direction*].
Over there. . . . Where did the sun go?

BOESMAN [*joining her*]. What you looking for?

LENA. Veeplaas.

BOESMAN. That way?

[*Lena studies Boesman's face for a second, then decides she is wrong.*]

LENA. No.

[*Moving in a different direction.*]
That way!

BOESMAN. Wrong!

[*Lena tries yet another direction.*]
Wrong!
Yessus, Lena! You're lost.

LENA. Do you really know, Boesman? Where and how?

BOESMAN. Yes!

LENA. Tell me.

[*He laughs.*]
Help me, Boesman!

BOESMAN. What? Find yourself?

[*Boesman launches into a grotesque pantomime of a search. Lena watches him with hatred.*]
[*Calling.*] Lena! Lena!
[*He rejoins her.*]
Sorry, Auntie. Better go to Veeplaas. Maybe you're there.

LENA [*directly at Boesman, her anger overwhelming her*].
Jou lae donner! Vark. Yes, you. You're a pig. *Voetsek*, you bastard. It's a sin, Boesman.

[*He enjoys her tirade immensely.*]
Wait a bit! One day . . . !

BOESMAN. One day what?

LENA. Something's going to happen.

BOESMAN. That's right.

LENA. What?

BOESMAN. Something's going to happen.

LENA. *Ja!*

[*Pause.*]

What's going to happen?

BOESMAN. I thought you knew. One day you'll ask me who you are.

[*He laughs.*]

LENA. *Ja*, another good laugh for you that day.

BOESMAN. The best one!

'*Ek sê, ou pellie* . . . who am I?' [*More laughter.*]

LENA [*trying her name*]. Lena . . . Lena. . . .

BOESMAN. What about Rosie? Nice name Rose. Maria. Anna. Or Sannie! Sannie who? *Sommer* Sannie Somebody.

LENA. NO!

BOESMAN [*ready to laugh*]. Who are you?

L'ENA. Mary. I want to be Mary. Who are you?

[*The laugh dies on Boesman's lips.*]

That's what I ask next. *Ja*, you! *Wie's die man?* And then I'm gone. Goodbye, darling. I've had enough. 'Struesgod, that day I'm gone.

BOESMAN. You mean that day you get a bloody *good* hiding.

LENA. *Aikona!* I'll go to the police.

BOESMAN. You tried that before and what happened? 'She's my woman, *baas*. *Net 'n bietjie warm gemaak.*' 'Take her' . . . finish *en klaar*. They know the way it is with our sort.

LENA. Not this time! My name is Mary, remember. 'Don't know this man, *baas*.' So where's your proof?

BOESMAN [*holding up a clenched fist*]. Here!

LENA. *Oppas!* You'll go too far one day. Death penalty.

BOESMAN. For you? [*Derisive laughter.*] Not guilty and discharge.

LENA. Don't talk big. You're frightened of the rope. When you stop hitting it's not because you're *moeg* or had enough. You're frightened! *Ja.*

[*Pause.*]

Ja. That's when I feel it most. When you do it carefully. The last few . . . when you aim. I count them. One . . . another one . . . wait for the next one! He's only resting.

[*Pause.*]

You're right, Boesman. That's proof. When I feel it I'll know. I'm Lena.

BOESMAN [*emphatically*]. And I'm Boesman.

LENA. Boesman and Lena.

BOESMAN. Yes! That's who. That's what. When . . . where . . . why! All your bloody nonsense questions. That's the answer.

LENA. Boesman and Lena.

BOESMAN. So stop asking them!

[*Pause . . . he goes back to work on the shelter. He tries the 'answer' for himself.*]

Boesman and Lena. *Ja!* It explains. So it's another *vrot ou huisie vir die vrot mens*. Look at it! Useless, hey. If it rains tonight you'll get wet. If it blows hard you'll be counting stars.

LENA. I know what it's like in there!

BOESMAN. It's all you'll ever know.

LENA. I'm sick of it.

BOESMAN. Sick of it! You want to live in a house? What do you think you are? A white madam?

LENA. It wasn't always like this. There were better times.

BOESMAN. In your dreams maybe.

LENA. What about Veeplaas? Chopping wood for the Chinaman? That room in his backyard. Real room, with a door and all that.

BOESMAN. Forget it. *Now* is the only time in your life.

LENA. No! 'Now.' What's that? I wasn't born today. I want my life. Where's it?

BOESMAN. In the mud, where you are, *Now*. Tomorrow it will be there too, and the next day. And if you're still alive when I've had enough of this, you'll load up and walk, somewhere else.

LENA. Roll up in my blanket and crawl into that! [*Pointing to the shelter.*]
Never enough wine to make us sleep the whole night. Wake up in the dark. The fire cold. What time is that in my life? Another 'now'! Black 'now' and empty as hell. Even when you're also awake. You make it worse. When I call you, and I know you hear me, but you say nothing. Sometimes loneliness is two . . . you and the other person who doesn't want to know you're there. I'm sick of you too, Boesman!

BOESMAN. So go.

LENA. Don't joke. I'll walk tonight. *So waar.*

BOESMAN. Go! Goodbye, darling.

[*Lena takes a few steps away from the fire then stops. Boesman watches her.*]

You still lost? Okay. Boesman will help you tonight. That way is Veeplaas. Through Swartkops, over the railway line, past that big thing with chimneys. Then you come to the veld. There's a path. Walk it until you see little lights. That's Veeplaas. Redhouse is that way. Korsten is over there. What else you want? Bethelsdorp? Coega Kop? There! There! I know my way. I know my world.

[*Lena is standing still.*]

So what you waiting for? Walk!

LENA [*her back to him, staring into the darkness*].
There's somebody out there.

[*Pause. Boesman leaves his work on the* pondok *and joins her. They stare in silence for a few seconds.*]

BOESMAN. Drunk.

LENA. No.

BOESMAN. Look at him!

LENA [*shaking her head*]. Nobody comes to the mudflats to get drunk.

BOESMAN. What do you know?

LENA. He's stopped. Maybe he's going to dig.

BOESMAN. Dark before the water's low.

LENA. Or a whiteman.

BOESMAN. When did you see a whiteman sitting like that!

LENA. Maybe he sees us.

[*She waves.*]

BOESMAN [*stopping her*]. What's the matter with you?

LENA. Go see what he wants.

BOESMAN. And then?

LENA. Do something. Help him.

BOESMAN. We got no help.

LENA. I'm not thinking of him.

[*Boesman stares at her.*]

It's another person, Boesman.

BOESMAN. I'm warning you! Don't start any nonsense.

[*He moves back to the shelter. Lena watches him for a few seconds, then decides.*]

LENA [*calling to the other person*].
Hey, I say.

BOESMAN. Lena!

LENA [*ignoring Boesman*]. We got a fire!

BOESMAN. Lena!

LENA. Come over!

BOESMAN. *Jou verdomde.* . . .

LENA [*sees the violence coming and moves away quickly*].
To hell with you! I want him.
[*Calling.*] Hey, darling! *Kom díe kant!*
[*To Boesman.*] Sit in the dark and talk to myself because you don't hear me any more? No, Boesman! I want him! Hey! He's coming.

[*A moment of mutual uncertainty at the approach of the stranger. Lena falls back to Boesman's side. He picks up a stick in readiness for trouble. They stand together, waiting.*
An old African appears slowly.
Hat on his head, the rest of him lost in the folds of a shabby old overcoat. He is an image of age and decrepitude.]

BOESMAN. *Kaffer!*

LENA. *Ou kaffer.*

[*Lena almost turns away with disappointment. Boesman sees this and has a good laugh.*]

BOESMAN. Lena calls out in the dark, and what does she get? Look at it.

LENA [*after a few more seconds of hesitation*].
Better than nothing.

BOESMAN. So? Go on. You wanted somebody. There's a black one.

[*Lena takes a few steps towards the old man. He has remained at a distance. As Lena approaches him he murmurs a greeting in Xhosa.**]

LENA. *Molo, Outa.*

[*Boesman watches this, and Lena's other attempts to communicate with the old man, with cruel amusement. She gets another murmur from the old man.*]

BOESMAN. What you waiting for?

LENA. I am Lena. This is my man, Boesman.

BOESMAN. Shake his hand! Fancy *Hotnot* like you. Give him some smart stuff. 'How do you do, darling.'

[*The old man murmurs something in Xhosa.**]

LENA. What's that? You know his language.

[*Boesman laughs.*]

Does the *Outa* want something?

[*Another murmur.*]

Don't you speak English or Afrikaans? '*Môre, baas!*'

BOESMAN. Give him some help.

LENA. He doesn't look so good.

[*A few steps closer to the old man.*]

Come sit, *Outa.* Sit and rest.

[*Nothing happens. She turns to Boesman.*]

How do you say that in the kaffir *taal*?

BOESMAN. *Hamba!*

LENA. All right, Boesman!

[*Back to the old man . . . she pushes forward a box.*]

It's warm by the fire.

[*Nothing happens . . . a spark of anger in her voice.*]

You deaf? Sit!

[*The old man does so.*]

Ja, rest your legs. They work hard for us poor people.

[*Boesman looks up in time to see her uncorking one of their bottles of water. They stare at each other in silence for a few seconds.*]

Maybe he's thirsty.

BOESMAN. And us?

LENA. Only water.

BOESMAN. It's scarce here.

LENA. I'll fetch from Swartkops tomorrow.

BOESMAN. To hell! He doesn't belong to us.

[*Grabs the bottle away from her and together with the other one puts it inside the* pondok.]

LENA. There was plenty of times his sort gave us water on the road.

BOESMAN. It's different now.

LENA. How?

BOESMAN. Because I say so.

LENA. Because this time you got the water, hey!

[*Back to the old man.*]

Does *Outa* come far?

[*She stands and waits. . . . Nothing.*]

We're from Korsten. They kicked us out there this morning.

[*Nothing.*]

It's a hard life for us brown people, hey.

BOESMAN. He's not brown people, he's black people.

LENA. They got feelings too. Not so, *Outa*?

BOESMAN. You'll get some feelings if you don't watch that fire.

[*Lena is waiting for a word from the old man with growing desperation and irritation.*]

LENA. What's the matter? You sick? Where's it hurt?

[*Nothing.*]

Hey! I'm speaking to you.

[*The old man murmurs in Xhosa.*]

Stop that baboon language! *Waar kry jy seer?*

[*Another unintelligible response.*]

162

[*Lena turns away in violent disgust.*] *Ag*, go to hell! *Onnooslike kaffer. My bleddy bek af praat vir niks!*

[*Boesman explodes into laughter at this ending to Lena's encounter with the old man.*]

BOESMAN. Finished with him already? *Ag nee, wat!* You must try something there. He's *mos* better than nothing. Or was nothing better?

Too bad you're both so useless. Could have worked a point. Some sports. You and him. They like *Hotnot meide.* Black bastards!

[*Lena is wandering around helplessly.*]

Going to call again? You'll end up with a tribe of old *kaffers* sitting here. That's all you'll get out of that darkness. They go there to die. I'm warning you, Lena! Pull another one in here and you'll do the rest of your talking tonight with a thick mouth. Turn my place into a *kaffer nes*!

LENA [*coming back dejectedly to the fire*].
Give me a *dop*.

BOESMAN. That's better. Now you're talking like a *Hotnot. Weg wêreld, kom brandewyn.*

LENA. A *dop*, please, man!

BOESMAN. You look like one too now. A real one. *Gat op die grond en trane vir 'n bottel.*

LENA [*really desperate*]. Then open one.

BOESMAN. All that fancy talk is thirsty work, hey.

LENA. Open a bottle, Boesman!

BOESMAN. When I'm ready.

LENA [*she stands*]. One of them is mine!

[*She waits for a reaction from Boesman, but gets none.*]
I want it now!

[*Pause.*]
I'm going to take it, Boesman.

[*She moves forward impulsively to where the bottles are hidden. Boesman lets her take a few steps then goes into action.*]

BOESMAN [*grabbing a stick*].
Okay!

LENA [*seeing it coming*].
Eina!

[*Running quickly to the old man.*]

Watch now, *Outa*. You be witness for me. Watch! He's going to kill me.

BOESMAN [*stopping*]. You asking for it tonight, Lena.

LENA. You see how it is, *Outa*?

BOESMAN. He'll see you get it if you don't watch out.

LENA. I got it this morning!

BOESMAN. Just touch those bottles and you'll get it again.

[*He throws down the stick and goes off.*]

LENA [*shouting after him*]. Go on! Why don't you hit me? There's no white *baases* here to laugh. Does this old thing worry you?

[*Turning back to the old man.*]

Look, *Outa*. I want you to look.

[*Showing him the bruises on her arms and face.*]

No, not that one. That's a old one. This one. And here. Just because I dropped the sack with the empties. I would have been dead if they hadn't laughed. When other people laugh he gets ashamed. Now too. I would have got it hard from him if you. . . .

[*Pause.*]

Why didn't you laugh? They laughed this morning. They laugh every time.

[*Growing violence.*]

What's the matter with you? *Kaffers* laugh at it too. It's *mos* funny. Me! *Ou meid* being *donnered*!

[*Pause. . . . She moves away to some small chore at the fire. After this she looks up at the old man, and then goes slowly to him.*]

Wasn't it funny?

[*She moves closer.*]

Hey, look at me?

[*He looks at her.*]

My name is Lena.

164

[*She pats herself on the chest. Nothing happens. She tries again, but this time she pats him.*]

Outa . . . You . . . [*patting herself*] . . . Lena . . . me.

OLD MAN. Lena.

LENA [*excited*]. *Ewe!* Lena!

OLD MAN. Lena.

LENA [*softly*]. My God!

[*She looks around desperately, then after a quick look in the direction in which Boesman disappeared, she goes to the half-finished shelter and fetches one of the bottles of water. She uncorks it and hurries back to the old man.*]

LENA [*offering the bottle*]. Water. *Water! Manzi!*

[*She helps him get it to his lips. He drinks. In between mouthfuls he murmurs away in Xhosa. Lena picks up the odd phrase and echoes it . . . 'Bhomboloza Outa, Bhomboloza' . . . 'Mlomo, ewe mlomo' . . . 'Yes, Outa, dala' . . . as if she understood him.*

The whole of the monologue follows this pattern: the old man murmuring intermittently—the occasional phrase or even sentence quite clear—and Lena surrendering herself more and more to the illusion of conversation.]

LENA. *Safa . . . safa. . . .*

[*Pause.*]

What's all that mean?

[*He hands her back the bottle.*]

If *Outa*'s saying. . . .

[*She stops, takes another quick look to make sure Boesman is out of sight, then returns to the old man's side. She speaks secretively and with intensity.*]

It's true! You're right. [*He is still murmuring.*] Wait now. Listen to mine.

I had a dog. In Korsten. Just a *brak*. Once when we were sitting somewhere counting our bottles and eating he came and looked at us. Must have been a *Kaffer hond*. He didn't bark. I left some bread for him there on the ground when we went. He ate it and followed us all the way back to Korsten.

[*Another look over her shoulder to make sure Boesman isn't near. She continues her story in an even lower tone.*]

For two days like that around our place there. When Boesman wasn't looking I threw him things to eat. Boesman knew I was up to something. I'm a bloody fool, *Outa*. Something makes me happy I start singing. So every time Boesman saw the dog, he throws stones. He doesn't like dogs. They don't like him. But when he wasn't looking I threw food.

[*Laughs secretively.*]

I won, *Outa*! One night the dog came in when he was asleep . . . came and sat and looked at me. When Boesman woke up, he moved out. So it was every night after that. We waited for Boesman to sleep, then he came and watched me. All the things I did—making the fire, cooking, counting bottles or bruises, even just sitting, you know, when it's too much . . . he saw it. *Hond!* I called him *Hond*. But any name, he'd wag his tail if you said it nice.

I'll tell you what it is. Eyes, *Outa*. Another pair of eyes. Something to see you.

Then this morning in all the *lawaai* and mix-up—gone!

I wanted to look, but Boesman was in a hurry.

So what! Now I got *Outa*.

[*Nudging him.*] Lena!

OLD MAN. Lena.

LENA [*little laugh*]. You see, I'm not ashamed.

Dè! [*In a fit of generosity she passes the bottle over again.*] Much as you like, darling. Doesn't cost a cent. Drink. Don't worry about him. He's worried about the wine. [*Old man drinks.*]

No heart in that one, *Outa*. Or empty. *Leeggesuip*. Tickey deposit for Boesman's heart. Brandy bottle.

[*She gets the bottle back and takes it to the* pondok, *talking all the time.*]

Outa know the empties. Brandy bottles, beer bottles, wine bottles. Any kind. Medicine. Tomato sauce. Sell them at the Bottle Exchange. We were doing good with the empties there in Korsten. Whiteman's drinking himself to death. Take your sack, knock on some back doors and it's full by no time. It was going easy for us, man. Eating meat. Proper chops! Then this morning: *Loop, Hotnot!* Just had time to grab our things. That's when I dropped the sack. Three bottles broken. I didn't even have on a *broek* or a petticoat when we started walking.

[*Straightens up at the shelter and registers the old man sitting quietly.*]
You're a nice *Ou* . . . [*correcting herself*] . . . you're one of the
good *Bantoes*, hey. I can see it. Sit so nice and listen to Lena.

[*Back to the fire where she puts on a few more pieces of wood.*]
That's why we called. I could see it. I said to Boesman: He's
one of the good ones. *Arme ou drommel!* Sorry feelings—for
you. 'Let's call him over!'

[*The old man starts murmuring again. This time it is accompanied
by much head-shaking. Lena interprets this as a rejection of what
she has just said.*]
No, *Outa*, I did! *Haai*, it's true! Why should I lie?

[*Her tone and manner becoming progressively more angry.*]
It's true! What do you know? Don't argue! Bloody old. . . .

[*The old man makes a move to stand up. Lena, changing tone and
attitude, forces him to stay seated.*]
Okay! Okay! Okay, *Outa*!! I'll tell you the truth. But mustn't
say I *lieg*. Sit still.

[*Pause.*]
It's my eyes. They're not so good any more, specially when
the thing is far away. But in the old days . . . ! You know
those mountains out there, when you walk Kleinskool way.
. . . In the old days so clear, *Outa*. When we were resting
I used to put my finger on a point, and then up and down,
just the way it is.

[*Demonstrates tracing the outline of a mountain range.*]
I haven't seen them for a long time. Boesman's back gets in
the way these days.

[*Breaking the mood.*]
It's not so bad, when the thing is near to me. Like Korsten,
this morning. That's quite clear. Tomorrow as well.
I can see that too, we'll be digging.
I say! *Ou* Lena's talking her head off tonight. And you sit
so nicely and listen to her. Boesman wouldn't. Tell me to
shut up.
[*Secretively.*] We must be careful. He'll try and chase you
away just now. Mustn't go, you see.

[*The old man starts murmuring again. For a few seconds Lena*

167

interprets it as small talk as she goes on preparing for their supper.]
That's right. Of course, *ja*, it's going to be cold tonight. You never said a truer thing, darling. I know, I know. Don't you worry. We'll eat just now. Won't take long to boil.

[*Pause. . . . The old man mumbles away, Lena studies him in silence for a few seconds.*]

LENA [*interrupting him*]. It's about Boesman, isn't it?

[*She laughs.*]

I *mos* know. Why shouldn't you and me talk? Well. . . . Too small for a real *Hotnot, Outa*. There's something else there. Bushman blood. And wild! That tickey deposit heart of his is tight, like his *poephol* and his fist.

[*Holds up a clenched fist in an imitation of Boesman.*]
That's how he talks to the world.

[*Much laughter from Lena at her joke, with a lot of nudging and back-slapping as if the old man was also laughing. He isn't.*]

Ja, so it goes. He walks in front. I walk behind. It used to be side by side, with jokes. At night he let me sing, and listened. Never learnt any songs himself.

[*The old man murmurs.*]

I don't know.

[*The old man continues to murmur, Lena gets desperate.*]

Don't start again, *Outa*. I don't know! Behind us. Isn't that enough? Too heavy to carry. The last time we joked, the last time I sang. Behind us somewhere. Our rubbish. We'll leave something here too if there's any last times left.
Yessus! It's so heavy now, *Outa*. Am I crooked? It feels that way when we stop and the bundles come down. What's so heavy? I walk and I think . . . a blanket, a few things in a bucket. . . .
Look! [*Pointing to their possessions.*]
And even when they're down, when you've made your place and the fire is burning and you rest your legs, something stays heavy. Hey! Once you've put your life on your head and walked you never get light again.
We've been walking a long time, *Outa*. Look at my feet.
Those little paths on the veld . . . Boesman and Lena helped write them.

I meet the memory of myself on the old roads. Sometimes young. Sometimes old. Is she coming or going? From where to where? All mixed up. The right time on the wrong road, the right road leading to the wrong place.

[*A murmur from the old man.*]

He won't tell me. That's a sin, isn't it? He'll be punished. But he says there's no God for us. Do you know? Up there!

[*A vague gesture to the sky. No intelligible response from the old man.*]

Doesn't matter.

[*The old man murmurs loudly, urgently.*]

What's that now? Maybe. . . .

[*Straightening up at the fire.*]

Yessus, Outa! You're asking things tonight. [*Sharply.*] Why do you want to know?

[*Pause.*]

It's a long story.

[*She moves over to him, sits down beside him.*]

One, *Outa,* that lived. For six months. The others were born dead.

[*Pause.*]

That all? *Ja.* Only a few words I know, but a long story if you lived it.

[*Murmuring from the old man.*]

That's all. That's all.

Nee, God, Outa! What more must I say? What you asking me about? Pain? Yes! Don't *kaffers* know what that means? One night it was longer than a small piece of candle and then as big as darkness. Somewhere else a donkey looked at it. I crawled under the cart and they looked. Boesman was too far away to call. Just the sound of his axe as he chopped wood. I didn't even have rags!

You asked me and now I've told you. Pain is a candle *entjie* and a donkey's face. What's that mean to you? You weren't there. Nobody was. Why do you ask *now?*| You're too late for that. *This* is what I feel now [*the fire, the shelter, her 'here and now'*]. . . . This!

My life is here tonight. Tomorrow or the next day that one

169

out there will drag it somewhere else. But tonight I sit *here*. You interested in that?

[*The old man gets slowly to his feet and starts to move away. Lena throws herself at him violently.*]

LENA. Not a damn! I'm not finished! You can't just go, walk away like you didn't hear. You asked me, and I've told you. This is what I'm left with. You've got two eyes. Sit and look!

[*She has forced the old man back on his box. Lena calms down.*]
Lena!

OLD MAN. Lena.

LENA [*trying to mollify him*]. I'll ask Boesman to give you a *dop*. Okay? Won't be too bad. Where could you go now? Dark out there, *Outa. Skelms* will grab you.

[*She hears a noise . . . moves away a few steps and peers into the darkness.*]

He's coming. Listen, we must be clever now. Don't look happy. And don't say anything. Just sit still. Pretend we're still *kwaai-vriende*.

[*She goes back to her fire. Another idea sends her back hurriedly to the old man.*]

No. I know what you do. When he comes back you must say you'll buy wine for us all tomorrow. Say you got a job in Swartkops and when you get your pay you'll buy wine. You hear me? [*Violently.*] Hey . . . !

[*Before she can say anything more, Boesman appears. He has a few more pieces of firewood, and something else for the shelter. Lena scuttles back to the fire, and makes herself busy. Boesman stops and stares at the two of them.*]

BOESMAN. What you been doing?

LENA [*innocently*]. Nothing. Look at the wine if you don't believe me.

BOESMAN. Then why's he still here?

LENA. I been looking after the fire. Water's nearly boiling.

BOESMAN. *You* called him . . . *you* tell him to go.

LENA [*looking furtively at the old man, waiting for him to speak*]. This wood doesn't mean much. Won't last the night.

BOESMAN. Don't pretend you didn't hear.

LENA. Okay.

[*Tries to lose herself in fussing with the pot.*]

[*Boesman waits.*]

BOESMAN. So when you going to tell him to go?

LENA. Who?

BOESMAN. Don't play stupid with me, Lena!

LENA. Him? Slowly there?

[*Leaves the fire and talks to him with an exaggerated show of secrecy.*]
He's okay.

BOESMAN. What's that mean?

LENA. Good *kaffer*.

BOESMAN. How do you know?

LENA [*to the old man*]. Tell him what you said to me, *Outa*.

BOESMAN. Since when can you speak his language?

LENA. He's got a few words of Afrikaans. *Outa!!*

BOESMAN. What did he say?

LENA. He said he's going to buy wine tomorrow.

[*To the old man.*] Not so?
He's got some jobs there in Swartkops. Some garden jobs.
Ask him.

BOESMAN. Who's going to give *that* a job?

LENA. Somebody with a soft heart.

BOESMAN. You mean a soft head.

LENA [*forcing a laugh*]. Soft head! Bloody good, Boesman.

BOESMAN. Garden job! He hasn't got enough left in him to
dig his own grave.

LENA. Soft heart and a soft head! *Haai!*

[*Lena is laughing too much. Boesman stares at her. She stops.*]

LENA [*weakly*]. Funny *ou grappie*.

[*Boesman's suspicions are aroused. He goes back to work on the shelter,
but watches the other two very carefully. Lena, thinking she has won,
starts to lay out their supper.*]

LENA [*pointing to a loaf of brown bread*]. Can I break it in three
pieces?

BOESMAN. Two pieces!

[*Lena wants to rebuke him, but stops herself in time.*]

LENA [*softly to the old man*]. We'll share mine.

[*Looks up to see Boesman watching her.*]

Pondokkie's looking okay. *Oulike ou nessie.* He's good with his hands, *Outa.*

[*Without realizing what she is doing, Lena starts humming a little song as she works away at the fire. She realizes her mistake too late. Boesman is staring hard at her when she looks up.*]

[*Desperately.*] I'm not happy!

BOESMAN. You're up to something.

LENA. 'Struesgod I'm not happy.

BOESMAN. He must go.

LENA. Please, Boesman!

BOESMAN. He's had his rest. Hey!

LENA. It's dark now.

BOESMAN. That's his troubles. Hey! *Hamba wena!*

LENA. He's not doing any harm.

BOESMAN. He'll bring the others. It's not far to their location from here.

LENA. Boesman! Just for once a favour. Let him stay.

BOESMAN. What's he to me?

LENA. For me, man. [*Pause.*] I want him.

BOESMAN. What for? What you up to, Lena?

[*Pause. . . . Lena can't answer his questions.*]

LENA [*impulsively*]. You can have the wine. All of it. Next time as well.

[*She dives to the shelter, produces the two bottles of wine.*]
There!

BOESMAN [*unbelievingly*]. For that!

LENA. I want him.

BOESMAN. This is wine, Lena. That's a *kaffer.* He won't help you forget. You want to sit sober in this world? You know what it looks like then?

LENA. I want him.

BOESMAN [*shaking his head*]. You off your mind tonight.
[*To the old man.*] You're an expensive *ou drol.* Two bottles of wine! *Ek sê.* Boesman has party tonight.

[*He tantalizes Lena by opening a bottle and passing it under her nose.*]

Smell! *Hotnot's* forget-me-not.

[*First mouthful.*]

Weg wêreld, kom brandewyn.

LENA [*restraining the old man*].

No, *Outa.* I've paid. You can stay the night with us. If we all lie together it will be warm in there.

BOESMAN [*overhearing*]. What do you mean?

LENA [*after a pause*]. You can have the mattress.

BOESMAN. To hell! He's not coming inside. Bring your *kaffer* and his fleas into my *pondok.* Not a damn.

LENA. He won't sit there by himself.

BOESMAN. Then sit with him!

[*He sees Lena's dilemma . . . enjoys it.*]

Ja! You can choose. Inside here or take your fleas and keep him company.

[*Pause. . . . Boesman works away, tries to whistle.*]

I said you can sleep inside with me or. . . .

LENA. I heard you, Boesman.

BOESMAN. So?

[*Lena doesn't answer. Boesman rubs it in.*]

It's going to be cold tonight. When it starts pushing and the water comes back. Boesman's all right. Two bottles and a *pondokkie. Bakgat!*

[*He watches Lena. She moves slowly to their things. For the first time he is unsure of himself.*]

What you going to do?

[*Lena doesn't answer. She finds one of their blankets and takes it to the old man.*]

LENA. Here, *Outa.* We'll need it.

BOESMAN [*suddenly on his feet*]. I've changed my mind. He must go.

LENA [*turning on him with unexpected ferocity*].

Be careful, Boesman!

BOESMAN. Of what?

LENA [*eyes closed, fists clenched*]. Be careful.

[*Her tone stops him. He sits down again, now even more unsure of himself.*]

BOESMAN. You think I care what you do? You want to sit outside and die of cold with a *kaffer*, go ahead!

LENA. I'd sit out there with a dog tonight!

[*Turns back to the old man.*]

We'll need more wood. And something in case it rains. I'm not so handy at making shelter, *Outa*.

[*To Boesman.*] Where did you find that stuff? Anything left out there?

[*This time Boesman doesn't answer. He stares at her with hard disbelief.*]

I'll see what I can find, *Outa*.

[*She wanders off. Boesman, in front of his shelter with the two bottles of wine, watches her go. When she has disappeared he studies the old man. Takes a few more swallows, then gets up and moves a few steps in the direction that Lena left. Certain that she is not about he turns and goes back to the old man.*]

BOESMAN [*standing over him.*] Hond!

[*The old man looks up at him. Boesman pulls the blanket away from him.*]

I want two blankets tonight.

[*Still not satisfied, he sends the old man sprawling with a shove. The old man crawls back laboriously to his seat. Boesman watches him, then hears Lena returning. He throws back the blanket.*]

If you tell her, I'll kill you.

Bulala wena!

[*He returns to his shelter, sits down, and continues drinking. He will remain in this position, watching Lena and the old man, until the end of the Act.*]

LENA [*a few small pieces of wood are all she has found*].
It's too dark now.

[*She goes to the fire. Their tea is now ready. She pours it into two mugs, taking one of them and half the bread to Boesman. Then she joins the old man with her share. She sits beside him.*]

As long as it doesn't rain it won't be so bad. The blanket

will help. Nights are long, but they don't last for ever. This wind will also get tired.

[*Her mug of tea and bread are placed before them.*]

It's a long time since we had somebody else with us. Sit close to the fire. That's it!

[*She throws on another piece of wood.*]

It won't last long, but it's big enough. Not much to see. This is all. This is mine.

Look at this mug, *Outa* . . . old mug, hey. Bitter tea, a piece of bread. Bitter and brown. The bread should have bruises. It's my life.

[*Passing him the mug.*]

There, don't waste time. It's still warm.

[*They drink and eat. Boesman is watching them from the shelter, his bread and tea untouched before him.*]

ACT TWO

An hour later.

Lena and the old man are still sitting together on the box, huddled together under the blanket. Boesman is on his legs in front of them, the second bottle of wine in his hands. Under the influence of the wine his characteristic violence is now heightened by a wild excitability.

His bread and tea are still untouched on the ground.

BOESMAN. Again.

LENA. No.

BOESMAN. Yes!

LENA. You said that was the last time.

BOESMAN. You didn't do it right.

LENA. Have a heart, Boesman. Leave us alone now, man!

BOESMAN. Come on! 'Please, *my baasie!*'
  [*Pause.*] Lena!

LENA [*giving in*]. ' Please, *my baasie.*'

BOESMAN. Properly. The way you did it this morning.

LENA. 'Please, *my baasie.*'

BOESMAN [*pointing to the old man*]. Him too. Hey!

LENA. Say it, *Outa.*

  [*The old man mumbles something.*]

BOESMAN. '*Ag siestog, my baas.*'

LENA. '*Ag siestog, my baas.*'

BOESMAN. No bloody good.

LENA [*reaching breaking-point, she jumps up*].
  Enough, Boesman!

BOESMAN. Not enough. Whiteman won't feel sorry for you.

LENA. Then you try!

BOESMAN. You must make the words crawl to him, with your tongue between their back legs. Then when the *baas* looks at you, wag it just a little . . . '*Siestoggies, my baas! Siestoggies, my groot* little *baasie!*'

LENA. Whiteman! Whiteman! Whiteman's dog. *Voetsek!*

  [*Boesman laughs.*]

  I'll pick up a stone, Boesman.

[*Boesman growls at her.*]

[*Sitting down beside the old man again.*] That's what he is, *Outa*. Make life hell for anything that smells poor. He's worse. They stop barking when you've walked past. This one's following me to my grave.

BOESMAN [*launching into a vulgar parody of Lena, with the appropriate servile postures and gestures*].
'*Sommer* a *ou* Hotnot, baas. Lena, baas. *Van ou* Coega, baas *Ja, my baas.*'

[*He turns on her.*]

You!

[*He extends the pantomime to a crude imitation of the scene that morning when the Korsten shacks were demolished.*]

[*Peering at something.*] '*En dit? Nee, moer!* Boesman. Hey, Boesman! *Daar kom 'n ding die kant.* Save our things! [*In and out of the shelter.*] Give us time, *my baas. Al weer sukke tyd.* Poor old Lena. Just one more load, *baas. Arme ou Lena!*'

[*Abandoning the act and turning on Lena again.*]

This morning! That's how you said it. That's what you looked like.

LENA. And did somebody feel sorry for us?

BOESMAN. The lot of you! Crawling out of your holes. Like worms. *Babalas* as the day you were born. That piece of ground was rotten with *dronkies.* Trying to save their rubbish, falling over each other . . . !

'Run you bastards! Whiteman's bulldozer is chasing you!'

[*Big laugh.*]

LENA. And then he hit me for dropping the empties.

BOESMAN [*the bulldozer*]. Slowly it comes . . . slowly . . . big yellow *donner* with its jawbone on the ground. One bite and there's a hole in the earth! Whiteman on top. I watched him. He had to work, *ou boeta.* Wasn't easy to tell that thing where to go. He had to work with those knobs!
In reverse . . . take aim! . . . *maak sy bek oop!* . . . then horsepower in top gear and smashed to hell. One push and it was flat. All of them. Slum clearance! And what did we do? Stand and look.

[Another imitation].

'*Haai! Kyk net. Witman is 'n snaakse ding.*'

[Boesman laughs.]

But the dogs knew. They had their tails between their legs. They were ready to run.

LENA. He laughed then too, *Outa*. Like a madman. Running around shouting and laughing at our own people.

BOESMAN. So would you if you'd seen them.

LENA. I did.

BOESMAN. You didn't. You were sitting there with our things crying.

LENA. I saw myself.

BOESMAN. And what did that look like?

LENA. Me.

BOESMAN. Only one.

LENA. One's enough.

BOESMAN. Enough! Leave that word alone. You don't know what it means.

LENA. It was the same story for all of us. Once is enough if it's a sad one.

BOESMAN. Sad story? Those two that had the fight because somebody grabbed the wrong *broek*? The *ou* trying to catch his donkey? Or that other one running around with his porridge looking for a fire to finish cooking it? It was bioscope, man! And I watched it. Beginning to end, the way it happened. *I* saw it. *Me.*
The women and children sitting there with their snot and tears. The *pondoks* falling. The men standing, looking, as the yellow *donner* pushed them over and then staring at the pieces when they were the only things left standing. I saw all that! The whiteman stopped the bulldozer and smoked a cigarette. I saw that too.

[Another act.]

'*Ek sê, my baas . . . !*' He threw me the *stompie*. '*Dankie, baas.*'

LENA. They made a big pile and burnt everything.

BOESMAN. Bonfire!

LENA. He helped drag what was left of the *pondoks*. . . .

BOESMAN. Of course. Full of disease. That one in the uniform told me. '*Dankie, baas!*'

LENA. Just like that.

BOESMAN [*violently*]. Yes! *Dankie, baas.*
You should have said it too, sitting there with your sad story. Whiteman was doing us a favour. You should have helped him. He wasn't just burning *pondoks*. They alone can't stink like that. Or burn like that.
There was something else in that fire, something rotten. Us! Our sad stories, our smells, our world! And it burnt, *boeta*. It burnt. I watched that too.
The end was a pile of ashes. And quiet.
Then . . . 'Here!' . . . then I went back to the place where our *pondok* had been. It was gone! You understand that? Gone! I wanted to call you and show you. There where we crawled in and out like baboons, where we used to sit like them and eat, our head between our knees, our fingers in the pot, hiding away so that the others wouldn't see our food. . . .
I could stand there! There was room for me to stand straight. You know what that is? Listen now. I'm going to use a word. Freedom! *Ja*, I've heard them talk it. Freedom! That's what the whiteman gave us. I've got my feelings too, sister. It was a big one I had when I stood there. That's why I laughed, why I was happy. When we picked up our things and started to walk I wanted to sing. It was Freedom!

LENA. You still got it, *ou ding*?

[*Boesman stares at her dumbly. He wanders around aimlessly, looking at the fire, the other two, the shelter, as if he were itemizing every detail in his present situation. Lena watches him.*]

You lost it?

[*Boesman doesn't answer.*]

Your big word? That made you so happy?

BOESMAN. When I turned off the road, when I said Swartkops. I didn't want to! Say it, or think it. Any of the old places. I didn't want to. I tried!
The world was open this morning. It was big! All the roads . . . new ways, new places. *Yessus!* It made me drunk.

Which one? When the robot said 'Go' there at Berry's Corner I was nearly *bang in my broek*.

LENA. So that's what we were looking for, that *dwaal* there in the back streets. Should have seen us, *Outa*! Down one, up the other, back to where we started from . . . looking for Boesman's Freedom.

BOESMAN. I had it!

It was you with your big mouth and stupid questions. 'Where we going?' Every corner! 'Hey, Boesman, where we going?' 'Let's try Veeplaas.' 'How about Coega?' All you could think of was those old rubbish dumps. 'Bethelsdorp . . . Mission-vale. . . .'

Don't listen to her, Boesman! Walk!

'Redhouse . . . Kleinskool. . . .'

They were like fleas on my life. I scratched until I was raw.

LENA. We had to go somewhere. Couldn't walk around Korsten carrying your Freedom for ever.

BOESMAN. Every time you opened your mouth it got worse.

LENA. Bad day for Lena. Three empties and Boesman's Freedom in pieces.

BOESMAN. By the time you shut up we just a *vlenterbroek* and his *meid* in the backyard of the world.

I saw that piece of *sinkplaat* on the side of the road, I should have passed it. Gone on! Freedom's a long walk.

But the sun was low. Our days are too short.

[*Pause.*]

Too late, Boesman. Too late for it today.

So I picked it up. Finish and *klaar*. Another *pondok*.

[*Shouting violently.*]

It's no use, *baas*. Boesman's done it again. Bring your bull-dozer tomorrow and push it over!

[*To the old man.*] Then you must run. It will chase you too. *Sa! Sa vir die kaffer!*

LENA. Don't listen to him, *Outa*. There's no hurry. When it's over they let you walk away. Nobody had to run. One by one we went, a few things on the head, different ways, one by one.

BOESMAN. Whiteman's wasting his time trying to help us.

Pushed it over this morning and here it is again. Push this one over and I'll do it somewhere else. Make another hole in the ground, crawl into it, and live my life crooked.
One push. That's all we need. Into gaol, out of your job . . . one push and it's pieces.
Must I tell you why? Listen! I'm thinking deep tonight. We're whiteman's rubbish. That's why he's so *beneukt* with us. He can't get rid of his rubbish. He throws it away, we pick it up. Wear it. Sleep in it. Eat it. We're made of it now. His rubbish is people.

LENA. Throw yourself away and leave us alone.

BOESMAN. It's been done. Why do you think we sit here like this? We've been thrown away. Rubbishes. Him too. [*Pointing to the old man.*] They don't want him any more. Useless. But there! You see what happens. Lena picks him up. Wraps him in a blanket. Gives him food.

LENA. You picked up yours. I picked up mine.

BOESMAN. I got mine for nothing. It made a *pondok*. What you going to do with him?

[*Pause.*]

Hey! I'm speaking to you. You paid a lot for that *ou drol*. Bottle of wine. You happy now?

LENA. I didn't buy *Outa* for happiness.

BOESMAN. So then what's the use of him? Is he hot stuff? Keeping you warm there?

LENA. No.

BOESMAN. You two up to something under that blanket?

[*Lena doesn't answer.*]

Lena and *ou* better-than-nothing. Waiting for me to go to sleep, hey. *Vuilgoed!*

LENA. No, Boesman.

BOESMAN. You're cold, you're hungry, you're not making Happiness but still you want him.

LENA. Yes.

BOESMAN [*turning away with a forced laugh*].
Nee, God! She's gone mad. Lena's gone mad on the mudflats. Sit there with a *kaffer*. . . .

[*His laughter spirals up into violent bewilderment. He faces her savagely.*]

Why?! Why?!!!

[*Pause.*]

LENA [*she takes her time*].

What we doing to you, Boesman? Why can't you leave us alone? You've had the wine, you've got the shelter. What else is there? Me?! *Haai*, Boesman, is that why he worries you? You jealous . . . because Lena's turned you down, your *pondok*, and your bottle?

Must I tell you why?

That's not a *pondok*, Boesman. [*Pointing to the shelter.*] It's a coffin. All of them. You bury my life in your *pondoks*. Not tonight. Crawl into darkness and silence before I'm dead. No! I'm on this earth, not in it.

Look now. [*She nudges the old man.*] Lena!

OLD MAN. Lena.

LENA. *Ewe*, Lena.

[*To Boesman.*] That's me.

You're right, Boesman. It's here and now. This is the time and place. To hell with the others. They're finished, and mixed up anyway. I don't know why I'm here, how I got here. And you won't tell me. Doesn't matter. They've ended *now*. The walks led *here*. Tonight. And he sees it.

BOESMAN. What's there to see? Boesman and Lena on the mudflats at Swartkops. Like any other night.

LENA. That's right.

BOESMAN. And tomorrow night will be the same. What you going to do then? Maybe I'll kick you out again.

LENA. You didn't kick me out.

BOESMAN. Tomorrow night I will. And you'll sit alone. Because he won't be here. That I tell you. Or anybody else.

LENA. He's here now.

[*Boesman leaves her and sits down in front of his shelter, drinking, in a withdrawn and violent silence.*]

[*To the old man.*] Not yet, *Outa*. [*Shaking him.*] It's not finished. Open your eyes.

[*To Boesman.*]

If you don't want your bread and tea pass it this way, man.

[*Boesman studies Lena in silence for a few seconds then stretches out a leg and pushes over the mug of tea. He watches Lena for a reaction. There is none. In a sudden fury he picks up the bread and hurls it into the darkness.*]

BOESMAN. I've told you, we've got no help.

[*Disappears into the shelter with his bottle of wine, reappears, on his knees, almost immediately.*]

I'm kicking you out *now*. Even if you change your mind you can't come in.

LENA. I won't, Boesman.

[*Boesman disappears into the shelter.*]

Maybe he'll sleep now.

[*The old man leans forward.*]

No, *Outa*, not us. [*Shaking him.*]

Listen to me. You'll never sleep long enough.

Sit close. *Ja! Hotnot* and a *Kaffer* got no time for apartheid on a night like this. We must keep that bit of wood for later. After that there's nothing left. Don't think about what you're feeling. Something else. Warm times. Let's talk about warm times. Good walk on a nice day! Not too long, not too hot. Otherwise you're back in hell again . . . as hot as this one's cold. In and out, hey, *Outa*, we poor people. But when it's just right! It's a feeling. And a taste, when you lick your lips. Dust and sweat.

Hard work too. Watch tomorrow. You start to dig for prawns, your hands are stiff, the mud and water is cold, but after a little while you start to sweat and it's okay.

Outa must help us dig tomorrow. Get nice and warm. And a good dance! *Yessus, Outa*. There's a warm feeling. If we had a *dop* inside now we could have tried. Hard to make party without a *dop*.

[*Humming.*] Da . . . da . . . da.

Outa know that one? *Ou Hotnot* dance. Clap your hands. So.

[*She starts clapping and singing softly.*]

'*Die trane die rol vir jou, bokkie!*'

Coegakop days! Lena danced the moon down and the sun up. The parties, *Outa*! Happy Christmas, Happy New Year,

Happy Birthday . . . all the Happies. We danced them. The sad ones too. Somebody born, somebody buried. We danced them in, we danced them out. It helps us forget. Few *dops* and a guitar and it's *voetsek* yesterday and to hell with tomorrow. [*Singing.*] Da . . . da . . . da . . . da. . . .
Outa's not clapping. So.
[*Clapping and singing.*] Da . . . da . . . da . . . da. . . .

> Ou blikkie kondens melk
> Maak die lewe soet ;
> Boesman is 'n Boesman
> Maar hy dra 'n Hotnot hoed.

Not like your dances. No war-dances for us. They say we were slaves in the old days. Just your feet on the earth and then stamp. Hit it hard!
[*Still seated, she demonstrates.*]
Da . . . da . . . da . . . da. . . .
Nothing fancy. We don't tickle it like the white people. Maybe it laughs for them. It's a hard mother to us. So we dance hard. Let it feel us. Clap with me.
[*Lena is now on her legs. Still clapping she starts to dance. In the course of it Boësman's head appears in the opening to the shelter. He watches her.*]
[*Speaking as she makes the first heavy steps.*]
So for Korsten. *So* for the walk. *So* for Swartkops. *This* time. *Next* time. *Last* time.

[*Singing.*]

> Korsten had its empties
> Swartkops got its bait
> Lena's got her bruises
> Cause Lena's a *Hotnot meid.*

> Kleinskool got prickly pears
> Missionvale's got salt
> Lena's got a Boesman
> So it's always Lena's fault.

> Coegakop is far away
> Redhouse up the river
> Lena's in the mud again
> *Outa's* sitting with her.

[*She stops, breathing heavily, then wipes her forehead with her hand and licks one of the fingers.*]

Sweat! You see, *Outa*, Sweat. Sit close now, I'm warm. You feel me? And we've still got that wood!

[*They huddle together again under the blanket. Boesman is watching from the shelter. He lets them settle down before speaking.*]

BOESMAN. I dropped the empties.

[*Lena looks at him, she doesn't understand.*]

This morning. When we had to clear out of the *pondok*. I carried the sack.

[*It takes Lena a long time.*]

I dropped it.

LENA. [*She understands now. She speaks quietly.*]

You said I did.

BOESMAN. Yes.

LENA. You blamed me. You hit me.

BOESMAN. Yes.

LENA [*to the old man*]. He wanted to count the bottles before we left. Three were broken. He stopped hitting when the whiteman laughed. Took off his hat and smiled at them. 'Jus' a *ou meid, baas*.' They laughed louder. [*Pointing to her bruises.*] Too dark to see them now. He's hit me everywhere.

[*Her arms open . . . looking down at her body. She has a sense of her frail anatomy. She feels herself.*]

Haai, Yessus! Look at it. *Pap ou borste, ribbetjies.*

[*She looks up at Boesman. He is still watching her from the shelter.*]

For nothing then. Why do you tell me now?

[*Pause. . . . He stares at her.*]

You want to hurt me again. Why, Boesman? I've come through a day that God can take back. Even if it was my last one. Isn't that enough for you?

[*Pause.*]

No.

Why must you hurt me so much? What have I really done? Why didn't you hit yourself this morning? You broke the bottles. Or the whiteman that kicked us out? Why did you hit me?

BOESMAN [*now out of the shelter*].
  Why do I hit you?

  [*He tries to work it out. He looks at his hands, clenches one, and smashes it into the palm of the other.*]
  Why?

LENA. To keep your life warm? Learn to dance, Boesman. Leave your bruises on the earth.

BOESMAN [*another blow*]. Why?

LENA [*still quietly*]. Maybe you just want to touch me, to know I'm here. Try it the other way. Open your fist, put your hand on me. I'm here. I'm' Lena.

BOESMAN. Lena!

  [*Another blow, the hardest. He looks at her and nods.*]
  Lena . . . and I'm Boesman.

LENA. Hit yourself!

BOESMAN [*holding up his palm*]. It doesn't hurt.

LENA [*the first note of outrage*].
  And when it's me? Does that hurt you?
  What have I done, Boesman? It's my life. Hit your own.

BOESMAN [*equally desperate, looking around dumbly*].
  Show it to me! Where is it? This thing that happens to me. Where? Is it the *pondok*? Whiteman pushed it over this morning. Wind will do it to this one. The road I walked today? Behind us! Swartkops? Next week it's somewhere else. The wine? Bottles are empty. Where is it?!!
  [*Pause.*]
  I look, and I see you. I listen, I hear you.

LENA. And when you hit . . . ?

BOESMAN. You. You cry.

LENA. You hear that too?

BOESMAN. Yes.

LENA [*now almost inarticulate with outrage*].
  Moer! Moer!
  Outa hear all that? Hey! [*She shakes him violently.*] You can't sleep now! [*Changing her tone, pleading.*] Please, *Outa*. Just a little bit longer. I'll put the wood on the fire.
  [*She does so.*]

Wake up. This is the truth now. Listen.

BOESMAN [*watching her*]. You have gone mad tonight.

LENA. He's got to listen!

BOESMAN. He doesn't know what you're saying. *You* must wake up!
You've wasted your time with him. You've been talking to yourself tonight the way you've been talking to yourself your whole life. You're dumb. When you make a hole in your face the noise that comes out is as good as nothing, because nobody hears it.

LENA. Say it in the *kaffertaal*. 'You hit me for nothing.' Say it!

BOESMAN. No.

LENA. Then let him see it.

[*She crawls to Boesman in an attitude of abject beggary.*]

Hit me. Please, Boesman. For a favour. My last one, 'strue's-god. Hit me now.

[*To the old man.*] I've shown you the bruises. Now watch.

[*Pause. . . . Boesman is staring at her with disgust.*]

What you waiting for? You don't need reasons. Let him see it. Hit me!

BOESMAN [*withering disgust*]. Sies.

LENA. Who?

BOESMAN. *SIES!*

LENA. Me?

[*This is too much for Lena. She wanders around vacantly, almost as if she were drunk.*]

Nee, God! Nee nee nee nee, God!

I've got the bruises . . . he did it, he broke the bottles, but I've got the bruises and it's *'Sies'* to me?

What have I done?

BOESMAN. He doesn't know what you're saying!

LENA. Look at me, *Outa* . . . Lena! Me.

BOESMAN. There's only me. All you've got is me and I'm saying *'Sies!'*

LENA [*beside the old man on the box . . . softly . . .*]. Outa?

BOESMAN. You think I haven't got secrets in my heart too?

187

That's mine. *Sies!* Small little word, hey. *Sies.*
But it fits.

[*Parodying himself.*] '*Ja, baas! Dankie, baas!*'
Sies, Boesman!

And you? Don't ask me what you've done. Just look. You
say you can see yourself. Take a good look tonight! Crying
for a bottle, begging for bruises.

Sies, Lena! Boesman and Lena, *sies!*
We're not people any more. Freedom's not for us.
We stood there under the sky . . . two crooked *Hotnots.*
So they laughed.
Sies wêreld!

All there is to say. That's our word. After that our life is
dumb. Like your *moer.* All that came out of it was silence.
There should have been noise. You pushed out silence. And
Boesman buried it. Took the spade the next morning and
pushed our hope back into the dirt. Deep holes! When I
filled them up I said it again : *Sies.*

One day your turn. One day mine. Two more holes somewhere. The earth will get *naar* when they push us in. And
then it's finished. The end of Boesman and Lena.

That's all it is, tonight or any other night. Two dead *Hotnots*
living together.

And you want him to look? To see? He must close his eyes.
That's what I'll say for you in the *kaffertaal.*
Musa khangela! Don't look! That's what you must tell him.
Musa khangela!

LENA. He can't hear you, Boesman.

BOESMAN. *Musa khangela!*

LENA. Don't shout. I'm alone.

BOESMAN. What do you mean?

LENA. He can't hear you.

BOESMAN. Then wake him up.

LENA. Does it look like sleep? *Outa's* closed his eyes. The old
thing must have been tired. I tried to keep them open, make
him look. When he closed them his darkness was mine.

[*Pause. . . . Boesman now realizes. Lena looks up at him.*]
Ja! He's dead.

BOESMAN. How do you know?

LENA. He let go. He was holding my hand. He grabbed it, held it tight, then he let go.

BOESMAN. Feel his heart.

LENA. He's dead, Boesman. His hand is empty.

BOESMAN [*unbelievingly*]. He didn't cry, or something. . . .

LENA. Maybe it wasn't worth it.

BOESMAN. *He* wasn't worth it. Bottle of wine! And now . . . ? Didn't last you long.

[*The bottle in his hand.*] Mine too. Finished.

[*Throws the bottle aside.*] There goes mine.

[*Pause. . . . He looks at Lena and the old man again.*]

Morsdood?

LENA. *Ja.*

BOESMAN [*walking away*]. All yours.

LENA. Help me put him down.

BOESMAN [*quickly*]. He's got nothing to do with me.

[*Sits down in front of his shelter, nervous and uncertain.*]

You wanted him. You called him to the fire.

LENA [*gently easing the body down*].

Hey, heavy! No wonder we get *moeg*. It's not just the things on your head. There's also yourself.

[*She moves away.*]

BOESMAN [*after a pause*]. And now? What's going to happen now?

LENA. Is something going to happen now?

BOESMAN. Dead man.

LENA. Only a *kaffer. Outa.* Didn't even learn his real name. He said mine so nicely. Sorry, *ou ding.* Sorry.

BOESMAN [*false indifference*]. *Ja,* well . . . *môre is nog 'n dag.* I'm tired. Low water early. We'll have to *woel* if we want prawns. I'm going to sleep.

[*Pause.*]

I said I'm going to sleep.

LENA. I heard you.

BOESMAN [*before disappearing into the shelter*]. He's got nothing to do with me.

LENA. '*Môre is nog 'n dag.*' Maybe, hey, *Outa*. Maybe. So that's all. Hold on for as long as you can, and then let go.

BOESMAN [*shouting from inside the shelter*].
What are you doing?

LENA. Put your hands on the things in your life. Yours were full. Mug of tea, piece of bread. . . . Me.
Somebody else. Touch them, hold them. . . .

BOESMAN [*his head appearing in the opening of the shelter*].
What you doing?

LENA [*looking at him*].
. . . or make a fist and hit them.

BOESMAN. You can't just sit there. You better do something.
[*Pause.*]
Listen to me, Lena!

LENA. Why must I listen to you?

BOESMAN [*coming out*].
This is no time for more bloody nonsense! It's serious.

LENA. When *you* want somebody to listen, it's serious.

BOESMAN. That! [*Pointing to the body.*]

LENA. *Outa* still worry you? *Haai*, Boesman. He's dead.

BOESMAN. Dead men are dangerous. You better get rid of it.

LENA. Real piece of rubbish now, hey. What must I do?

BOESMAN. I don't give a damn. Just do it.

LENA. How do you throw away a dead *kaffer*?

BOESMAN. Your problems. He's got nothing . . .

LENA. . . . to do with you. Go back to sleep, Boesman.

BOESMAN. I am! Why must I worry? I did nothing. Clear conscience! Come and do his nonsense here! This is my place. I was here first. He should have stayed with his own sort. Then when I wanted to get rid of him, *you* stopped me.
[*There is no response from Lena to Boesman's growing agitation. This provokes him even more.*]
Are you a bloody fool?

LENA. You say so.

BOESMAN. That's big trouble lying there.

LENA. His troubles are over.

BOESMAN. And ours? What do you think is going to happen tomorrow?

LENA. I don't care.

BOESMAN. Well, I'm just warning you, you better have answers ready. Dead man! There's going to be questions.

LENA. About him? About rubbish? Hey, hey, hey! *Outa* hear that. '*Môre is sommer* a special *dag.*' They're going to ask questions!
About you! Hot stuff, hey. 'What's his name?' 'Where's he come from?'

BOESMAN. Never saw him before in my life!

LENA. 'Who did it?'

BOESMAN [*sharply*]. Did what? He died by himself.

LENA. Too bad you can't tell them, *Outa.*

BOESMAN. I did nothing.

LENA. Why don't they ask some questions when we're alive?

BOESMAN [*interrupting her*]. Hey! You saw.

LENA. What did I see?

BOESMAN. I did nothing to him. You saw that.

LENA. Now you want a witness too.

BOESMAN. I didn't touch him. You tell them.

LENA. What?

BOESMAN. The truth.

LENA. You got some words tonight, Boesman. Freedom. Truth. What's that? *Sies?*

BOESMAN. Stop your jokes, Lena! When they come tomorrow you just tell them. I was minding my own business. I only come here to dig for prawns.

LENA. Teach me again, Boesman. You *mos* know how the whiteman likes to hear it.
'He's just a *Hotnot, baas.* Wasn't doing any harm.' How's that? Will that make him feel sorry for you?

BOESMAN. Then the *kaffer* came. And *you* called him to the fire.

LENA. '*Siestoggies, my baas.*'

BOESMAN. I didn't want him. I didn't touch him.

LENA. 'Boesman didn't want him, *baas.*'

BOESMAN. I hate *kaffers.*

LENA. 'He hates *kaffers, baas.*'

BOESMAN. NO!!

LENA. 'He loves *kaffers, baas.*'

BOESMAN. God, Lena!

[*He grabs a bottle and moves violently towards her. He stops himself in time. Lena has made no move to escape or protect herself.*]

LENA. *Ja*, got to be careful now. There's one already.

[*Boesman is now very frightened. Lena watches him.*]

Whiteman's dog, his tail between his legs because the *baas* is going to be cross. *Yessus!* We crawl, hey. You're right, Boesman. And beg. 'Give us a chance.' *Siesiog.* I'm sorry for you. Hey. Maybe he's not dead.

[*Boesman looks at her.*]

That's a thought, hey! Maybe he's not dead, and everything is still okay.

BOESMAN. You said he was.

LENA. You believe me? You mean you're listening to Lena tonight. Are we talking to each other?

BOESMAN. Is he dead?

[*Lena laughs softly. Boesman moves uncertainly towards the body, unable to ignore the possibility with which she is tormenting him. He looks down at the dead man.*]

LENA. Go on.

BOESMAN. Wake up!

LENA. Doesn't speak our language, remember.

BOESMAN. Hey!

LENA. That's better.

BOESMAN [*nudging the body with his foot*]. *Vuka!*

LENA. Didn't he move there? Imagine he stands up now? Happy days! Dig prawns tomorrow, buy another bottle, give me a hiding.

[*Boesman is hesitating, uncertain of what to do next.*]

Feel his heart.

[*The nudge becomes a kick.*]

Much better. Let him feel your foot.

BOESMAN. Get up!

LENA. Don't let him play stupid with you. Make him get up. Tell him to go.

BOESMAN. *Voetsek!*

LENA. Louder! These *kaffers* are *onnooslik.*

BOESMAN [*his violence building up—another kick*]. Go die in your own world!

LENA. *Nog 'n een!*

[*Pause. . . . Boesman, rigid with anger and hatred, stares down at the inert body.*]

No bloody good. He's dead. And you, *ou boeta*, you're in trouble!

BOESMAN [*his control breaking*]. Bloody fool!

[*He falls to his knees and beats the body violently with his fists. Lena watches in silence. When Boesman is finished he goes back to his place in front of the shelter.*]

LENA. So that's how you do it. I know what it feels like. Now I know what it looks like. What do you think about, in between when you rest? Where to hit next?

[*Boesman is breathing heavily.*]

Hard work to beat the daylights out like that. Too bad there wasn't any left in him. *Outa's* in darkness. He won't be sore tomorrow, sit and count his bruises in the light. But he'll have them. When you hit me I go blue.

[*Pause.*]

You shouldn't have hit him, Boesman. Those bruises! Finger-prints. Yours. On him. You've made it worse for yourself. Dead *kaffer* and a *Hotnot meid* with bruises . . . and Boesman sitting near by with no skin on his knuckles. What's that look like? The answer to all their questions. They won't even ask them now. They'll just grab you . . . [*carefully*] . . . for something you didn't do!

That's the worst. When you didn't do it. Like the hiding you gave me for dropping the empties. Now you'll know what it feels like. You were clever to tell me. It hurt more

than your fists. You know where you feel that one? Inside.
Where your fists can't reach. A bruise there!
Now it's your turn!

[*Boesman, barely controlling his growing panic, gets stiffly to his legs.
He looks around . . . the dead man, Lena, the darkness . . . then
makes up his mind and starts to collect their things together.*]

BOESMAN. Come!

[*Lena doesn't respond.*]

On your legs! We're going.

LENA. *Haai*, Boesman! This hour! Where?

[*Boesman doesn't answer.*]

You don't know again, do you? Just crawl around looking
for a way out of your life.

Why must I go with you? Because you're Boesman and I'm
Lena?

BOESMAN [*urgently packing up their belongings . . . rolling blanket,
etc.*]

Are you coming? It's the last time I ask you.

LENA. No. The first time I tell you. No.

I've walked with you a long way, *ou ding*! It's finished now.
Here, in the Swartkops mud. I wanted to finish it this morning,
sitting there on the pavement. That was the word in my
mouth. NO! Enough! I wasn't ready for it yet. I am now.

[*Boesman is staring at her.*]

Don't you understand? It's over.

Look at you! Look at your hands! Fists again. When Boesman
doesn't understand something, he hits it.

You didn't understand him [*pointing to the dead man*], did you?
I chose him! A *kaffer*! Then he goes and buggers up everything by dying. So you hit him. And now me.

'No, Boesman! I'm not going with you!'

You want to hit me, don't you?

[*Barely controlling his panic now, Boesman goes on packing.*]

Run! It's trouble. Life's showing you bullets again. So run.
But this time you run alone. When you think you're safe
don't rest and wait for me to find you. I'm not running the
other way that leads me back to you. I'm not running at all.
I'm *moeg*. When you're gone I'll crawl in there and sleep.

[*Boesman stops his packing and looks up at Lena. He realizes her intention.*]

BOESMAN. That's what you think!

[*Boesman starts to smash the shelter with methodical and controlled violence.*]

LENA. *Hotnot* bulldozer! Hey, hey!

[*Jumps to her legs and prances around.*]

Dankie, baas Boesman! Smash it to hell! This is my laugh. Run, you old bastard. Whiteman's chasing you!

BOESMAN [*the shelter is totally demolished. He collects their things together with renewed energy.*]

Don't think I'm leaving you anything.

LENA [*pursuing him ruthlessly*].

Take the lot!

[*Helping him collect it all together.*] This . . . this. . . .

Don't forget my blanket.

[*It is still wrapped around the dead man. Boesman hesitates.*]

You frightened? There!

[*She pulls it off and throws it at Boesman.*]

Everything! I want boggerall. It's my life but I don't want to feel it any more. I've held on tight too long. I want to let go. I want nothing!

What's your big word? Freedom! Tonight it's Freedom for Lena. Whiteman gave you yours this morning, but you lost it. Must I tell you how? When you put all that on your back. There wasn't room for it as well.

[*All their belongings are now collected together in a pile.*]

You should have thrown it on the bonfire. And me with it. You should have walked away *kaal*!

That's what I'm going to be now. *Kaal*. The noise I make now is going to be new. Maybe I'll cry!! . . . Or laugh? I want to laugh as well. I feel light. Get ready, Boesman. When you walk I'm going to laugh! At you!

[*Boesman is loading himself up with their belongings . . . blankets, mattress, boxes. It is a difficult operation, the bundles are awkward, things keep falling out. But he finally manages to get it all on his back and under his arms. He stands before Lena, a grotesquely overburdened figure.*]

Eina! Look at you. *Here*, Boesman, the roads, going to be long tomorrow. And hard. You'll sweat.

What way you walking? Veeplaas? Follow the sun, that's where it goes. Sand between your toes tomorrow night.

[*Violently.*] So what you waiting for? Can't we say goodbye? We'll have to do it one day. It's not for ever. Come on. Let's say it now. Goodbye! Okay, now go. Go!! Walk!!

[*Lena turns her back on him violently and walks away. Boesman stands motionless. She ends up beside the old man.*]

Outa, why the hell you do it so soon? There's things I didn't tell you, man. And now this as well. It's still happening!

[*Softly.*] . . . *Moer moer moer.* Can't throw yourself away before your time. Hey, *Outa.* Even you had to wait for it.

[*She gets up slowly and goes to Boesman.*]

Give!

[*He passes over the bucket.*]

Hasn't got a hole in it yet. Might be whiteman's rubbish, but I can still use it.

[*It goes on to her head.*]

Where we going? Better be far. Coegakop. That's our farthest. That's where we started.

BOESMAN. Coega to Veeplaas.

LENA [*slowly loading up the rest of her share*].
First walk. I always remember that one. It's the others.

BOESMAN [*as Lena loads*]. Veeplaas to Redhouse. On *baas* Robbie's place.

LENA. My God! *Ou baas* Robbie.

BOESMAN. Redhouse to Missionvale . . . I worked on the salt-pans. Missionvale to Bethelsdorp.

Back again to Redhouse . . . that's where the child died. Then to Kleinskool. Kleinskool to Veeplaas. Veeplaas to here. First time. After that, Redhouse, *baas* Robbie was dead, Bethelsdorp, Korsten, Veeplaas, back here the second time. Then Missionvale again, Veeplaas, Korsten, and then here, now.

LENA [*pause. . . . she is loaded*].
Is that the way it was? How I got here?

BOESMAN. Yes.

LENA. Truly?

BOESMAN. Yes.

[*Pause.*]

LENA. It doesn't explain anything.

BOESMAN. I know.

LENA. Anyway, somebody saw a little bit. Dog and a dead man.

[*They are ready to go.*]

I'm alive, Boesman. There's daylights left in me. You still got a chance. Don't lose it. Next time you want to kill me, do it. Really do it. When you hit, hit those lights out. Don't be too late. Do it yourself. Don't let the old bruises put the rope around your neck. Okay. But not so fast. It's dark.

[*They look around for the last time, then turn and walk off into the darkness.*]

GLOSSARY

African and Afrikaans words and phrases are printed in bold, others in bold italic type. I would like here to acknowledge the assistance of Dr Elizabeth Gunner and the Reverend Barney Pityana in the compilation of this Glossary.

Ag: exclamation, roughly equivalent to 'oh', and pronounced like German *'ach'*

Ag nee, wat!: exclamatory, literally 'oh no, what!'

Ag siestog, my baas!: exclamatory, literally 'oh pity, my master' (see also **Sies**)

Ai: exclamation, expressing pain, as in 'ah', or 'ow'

Aikona: see **Haaikona**

Aina!: see **Eina!**

Aitsa! exclamation, 'whoops!'

Al weer sukke tyd: roughly equivalent to 'here we go again'

Arme ou drommel: 'poor old thing'

Arme ou Lena **se maer ou bene**: 'poor old Lena's skinny old legs'

Baas(es), Baasie: 'boss(es)' or 'master(s)'; familiarly, 'little boss/master' (*-ie* is the diminutive)

Babalas!: slang derived from Zulu *i-babalazi*, 'hung-over'

Bakgat!: slang, 'great!'

Bang in my broek: 'shit-scared', literally 'scared in my pants'

Bantoe(s), Bantu: official terms for black South Africans and their languages, disliked by them

Bedonnerd: see **Donner**

Beneukt: 'unreasonable, crazy; fed up'

Bhomboloza Outa, Bhomboloza: 'cry out, old man, cry out', from the Xhosa *ukubhomboloza*.

Bioscope: South African English, 'cinema'

Blikkie kondens melk: 'tin of condensed milk'

Blourokkie: prison slang for long-term prisoner; literally, 'blue dress', the colour of their uniform

Boer: 'farmer'

Boesman: derogatory term for a person of mixed-race, from Afrikaans for 'Bushman', as the Khokhoi people were formerly referred to

Boet, Boetie: 'brother'; 'little brother'; but also used to address a friend colloquially, as, e.g., 'pal'

Boggerall: South African English slang, 'buggerall'

Bokkie: 'little buck'; term of endearment

Boot: i.e. 'trunk' (US)

Brak: 'mongrel'

Broek: 'pants'; 'trousers'

Bulala wena!: 'I'll kill you!', a corruption of the Xhosa *ngizobulala wena!*

Capie: a 'Cape Coloured', i.e. person of mixed race

Chick-a-doem, doem, doem: onomatopoeic for a fast tune

Coolie: derogatory term for an Indian

Daar kom 'n ding díe kant: literally, 'there's a thing coming this way, this side'; 'something's coming'

Dala: see **Outa, dala**

Dankie, baas!: 'thank you, boss/ master!'

Dè!: 'there!', possibly from Zulu *kude*, 'far', if not simply English

Die geraas van 'n vervloekte lewe: 'the noise of a cursed life'

Die trane die rol vir jou, bokkie!: 'I'm crying for you, baby', literally, 'the tears roll for you, little buck'

Doek: 'head-scarf', as worn by black South Africans

Dominee: a minister of the Dutch Reformed Church; 'reverend' or 'minister'

Donner: (verb) 'beat up'; (noun) 'bastard'; thus also *bedonnerd* as an adjective, 'bloody' (abusive slang); derived from *donder*, 'to thrash'

Dop: 'tot' or drink of (hard) liquor

Drol: 'turd'

Dronkies: 'drunks'

Dwaal: 'to be in a *dwaal*', i.e. 'disoriented', 'confused'

Eina!: exclamation of pain, 'ow!'; similarly *Aina!*

Ek sê!: exclamation, 'hey!', literally 'I say!'

Ek sê, ou pellie: elaboration of above: 'hey, pal'

En dit? Nee, moer!: 'and that? No, fuck!' see also **Moer**

En klaar: as in 'finish *en klaar*'; emphatic expression, 'that's that'; 'finished and done with'

Entjie: 'stub-end' (of a cigarette); 'little piece'

Ewe: 'yes' (Xhosa)

G.M.: General Motors

Gat op die grond en trane vir 'n bottel: 'backside on the ground and crying for a bottle' (drink)

Gebabbel: 'babble'

Goosie: South African English slang term of endearment, 'cutie'

Haai!: exclamation of surprise, 'no!', 'well, I never!', from Xhosa *hayi*

Haaikona: emphatic negative, 'no, never', 'oh, no', etc., sometimes given as *aikona*; from Xhosa (and Zulu) *hayikhona*

Haai! Kyk net. Witman is 'n snaakse ding: 'no! Just look. The white man is a funny thing'

Hamba!: 'go!' from Nguni (Xhosa, Zulu) imperative, *ukuhamba*, often used offensively by non-Africans

Hamba wena!: 'push off!', 'get out, you!'; stronger and more insulting than *hamba*

Here: 'Christ', 'oh Lord', colloquial Afrikaans

Hoe's dit vir 'n ding!: 'how's

that!', 'how do you like that!'

Hoer: 'whore' (noun and verb)

Hond: 'dog'

Hotnot: corrupt form of 'Hottentot', term formerly used of San tribespeople, now abusive

Ja: 'yes'

Jou lae donner!: 'you dirty bastard'; see also **Donner**

Jou moer!: very obscene: 'you cunt!' (from *moer*, 'womb')

Jou verdomde . . .: 'you damned . . .'

Kaal, Kaalgat: 'naked', literally 'bare-arsed'

Kaffer: 'kaffir', abusive term for African; 'nigger' (US); hence also *Kaffermeid!*, 'Kaffir woman' and *kaffertaal*, 'kaffir language'

Klaar: 'finished', 'ready'; see **En klaar**

Klap: 'clout', 'blow'

Kom díe kant!: 'come here!', 'on this side!'

Kondens melk: 'condensed milk'

Koppies: 'little hills'

Kwaai-vriende: '"bad" friends', 'not on speaking terms'

Lawaai: 'noise', 'row'

Leeggesuip: 'empty', literally 'drunk dry'

Lieg: 'lie' (noun and verb)

Liewe God!: exclamation, 'dear God!'

Links draai, regs swaai: 'turn left, swing right'

Location: segregated area on outskirts of town or city set aside for African or 'Coloured' occupation, as in, e.g.,

Korsten location, Port Elizabeth; see also 'township'

Loop, Hotnot!: 'bugger off!', literally 'run, Hottentot'; see **Hotnot**

Luisgat!: 'louse' (*-gat*, or 'arse' reinforces the abusive meaning)

Maak sy bek oop!: 'open its mouth!' (*bek* is applied to animals, or abusively to humans)

Maer: 'thin'

Manzi!: 'water!' a corruption of Zulu *amanzi*

Meid: 'girl'; 'servant-woman'

Mlomo, ewe mlomo: 'mouth, yes, mouth', from the Xhosa

Moeg: 'worn-out', 'exhausted'

Moenie skiet, baas!: 'don't shoot, master!'

Moer!: obscene exclamation, 'fuck!'; 'womb'; see also **Jou moer!**

Molo, outa: 'hello, old man' (Xhosa); see **Outa**

Môre, baas!: 'good-day, master', from *môre*, meaning 'morning' or 'morrow', hence—

Môre is nog 'n dag: 'tomorrow is another day'

Morsdood: 'stone dead'

Mos: 'just'

Musa khangela!: 'don't look!', from Zulu *ukhangela*

My baasie: 'my master' (familiar)

Naar: 'queasy', 'sick'

Nee, God!: 'no, God!'

Nes: 'haunt' (noun), as in *kaffer nes*

Net 'n bietjie warm gemaak: 'just warmed up a little'

Nog 'n een: 'another one'

Onnooslik: 'stupid', 'witless'

Onnooslike kaffer. My bleddy bek af praat vir niks!: 'stupid "kaffir". To talk my bloody jaw off for nothing!'

Oppas: 'be careful', 'look out'

Opskud en uitkap: to dance fast, literally 'get up and get moving'

Ou: common mode of address to man or boy; 'chap', 'bloke'; also adjectival, meaning 'old' (see below)

Ou blikkie kondens melk: Old tin of condensed milk

    Maak die lewe soet: Makes life sweet;

    Boesman is 'n Boesman: Boesman is a Bushman

    Maar hy dra 'n Hotnot hoed: But he wears a Hottentot hat.

Ou boeta: mode of address to an elder brother, also to an old (i.e. long-term) friend

Ou ding: 'old thing'

Ou drol: 'old turd'

Ou grappie: 'silly little joke'

Ou hoer!: 'whore'

Ou Hotnot meid: 'Hottentot servant-woman'

Ou kaffer: 'old "kaffir"'

Oulike ou nessie: 'cute little nest'

Ouma: 'grandmother', but also a mode of address to an older woman

Ou meid: elderly servant-woman, presumed 'Coloured'

Ou pellie: 'pal'

Ou *Sister*: term of familiarity towards woman belonging to a 'sisterhood'; literally, 'old' sister

Outa: mode of address to an elderly, usually 'Coloured' or African man, often by children as a mark of respect to an elderly servant; derived from *ou + ta* (Xhosa, Zulu), 'old' + 'father'

Outa, dala: 'old man, old man', from 'outa' and Xhosa *mdala*, old man

P.E.: Port Elizabeth

Pap nat: 'sodden'

Pap ou borste, ribbetjies: 'flabby old breasts, thin little ribs'

Poep: 'fart'

Poephol: 'arse-hole'

Pondok, pondokkies: 'hut', 'shack'; 'little lean-tos'

Poopy: South African English slang, 'terrified'

Robot: South African English, 'traffic lights'

S.A.R.: South African Railways

Sa! Sa vir die kaffer!: 'Get him! After the "kaffir"'; used when setting a dog on someone or something

Safa: 'suffer' in Africanized pronunciation

Shame!: South African English, colloquial, 'poor thing!'

Sies: exclamation of disgust, 'ugh'

Siestoggies, my baas! Siestoggies, my groot *little* baasie!: expression of sympathy or dismay, 'ah, no, my master! No, my big little master!'

Sies wêreld!: expression of disgust towards the world

Sinkplaat: corrugated iron

Skeef: 'skew', 'crooked'

Skelms: 'rascals', 'rogues'

Skof: 'stretch' in the sense of the leg of a journey

Skop: 'kick' (noun and verb)

Skop and skip: 'hop and skip'

Skrik: 'fright'

Sleep: 'drag', 'pull along'

Soeterigheid: 'sweetness'

Sommer: 'just', 'simply'

Sommer *a* ou Hotnot, baas . . . **Van ou *Coega*, baas. Ja, my baas**: 'Just an old Hottentot, master . . . From old Coega, master. Yes, my master'

So waar: 'truly'

Stompie: 'cigarette-butt'

Stinkwood: wood of an indigenous hardwood tree, so named after the odour released when cut

Sukkel: 'struggle', 'toil'

Swartgat: abusive name for black South African, literally, 'black-arse'

Taal: 'language'

Tickey: name for obsolete South African threepenny piece, now superseded by five-cent coin; small coin

***Tickey*-draai**: lively country dance

Township: area set aside solely for 'Coloured' or African occupation, e.g. New Brighton township

Vark: term of abuse, 'pig'

Vastrap: fast country dance, literally 'quick-step'

Vat jou goed en trek!: 'take your things and go!'

Vies!: 'angry!', 'disgusted!'

Vlenterbroek: 'torn trousers'

Voetsek!: rough command to go, usually to a dog, offensive to a person, equivalent to 'bugger off!'

Vrot!: 'no good', 'rotten'

Vrot ou huisie vir die vrot mens: literally, 'rotten little old house for rotten people'

Vuilgoed!: 'rubbish!', 'garbage!'

Vuka!: 'arise!', 'wake up!', Nguni (Zulu and Xhosa)

Waar die donner is . . . ?: 'where the hell is . . . ?', see also **Donner**

Waar kry jy seer?: 'where does it hurt (you)?'

Weg wêreld, kom brandewyn: 'go away world, come brandy'

Wie's die man?: 'who's that man?'

Witman is 'n snaakse ding: see **Haai!**

Woel: 'hurry', 'get a move on'

Yessus!: 'Jesus!'